The Symphony of Truth

The Symphony of Truth

SERAFINO M.
LANZETTA

The Symphony of Truth

Theological Essays

AROUCA PRESS

Copyright © Arouca Press 2021
Copyright © Serafino M. Lanzetta

All rights reserved:
No part of this book may be reproduced or transmitted,
in any form or by any means, without permission

ISBN: 978-1-989905-50-0 (pbk)
ISBN: 978-1-989905-51-7 (hardcover)

Arouca Press
PO Box 55003
Bridgeport PO
Waterloo, ON N2J3G0
Canada
www.aroucapress.com
Send inquiries to info@aroucapress.com

Book and cover design by
Michael Schrauzer

CONTENTS

Introduction ix

1 The Sacrament of Matrimony as the
  Spousal Love of Christ for His Church 1
2 *Amoris Laetitia*: The Joy of Love that
  Divides the Church 19
3 Nominalism: The Great Temptation of These Days . . 43
4 Martin Luther 500 Years Later:
  Prophet or Revolutionary? 51
5 Vatican II: A Pastoral Challenge & the
  Key-Problem of its Hermeneutics 67
6 The Renewal of the Permanent Diaconate
  in the Second Vatican Council 83
7 The Theological Importance of *Humanæ Vitæ*
  and Its Prophecy for Our Time 101
8 To the Root of Today's Church Crises:
  A Theological Collapse 115
9 The Uneasy Path from *Gaudium et Spes*
  to *Humanæ Vitæ* 121
10 A 'Sacerdotal People of God':
   A Look at the Priesthood of Mary and
   Her Victimhood as Co-Redemptrix 125

INTRODUCTION

During the last years of my ministry in the UK, I began to think in English, which is not an easy thing for an Italian man! Freed from the linguistic barrier, I was able to reach a new audience of English speakers. I began presenting theological talks and writing essays for magazines or websites. While compiling all of this material into a book, it became clear that I needed to find a golden thread, tying all theological themes together and tracing their origin back to a single Truth.

Theology is in fact the *intellectus fidei*—the intelligence of the one faith, the same yesterday and today, composed of distinct but analogical mysteries. The truth is symphonic, as Hans Urs von Balthasar says. It is like one piece of music played by many instruments. The greater the variety of instruments playing the same piece, the better they express the beauty of that one musical score. The same should be true of the multitude of believers around the world. If this is not the case, there is some lack, not in the mystery, but in the approach to the faith. The role of a single instrument is only clear within the context of the whole symphony. Similarly, it is only within the context of the whole faith, starting with the faith of the Church, that one can distinguish the peculiarity of a single mystery. This is what I tried to do by bringing together individual tiles of theology—theological opinions offering an interpretation of dogma and its defence when necessary, holding on as close as possible to revealed dogma—in order to compose one grand mosaic.

Starting in the first essay with the mystery of holy matrimony established by God the Creator and the Redeemer—a natural indissoluble pact elevated to the dignity of sacrament—I proceed in the second essay to discuss the theological problems ignited by *Amoris Laetitia*, the post-synodal Exhortation of Pope Francis on family life. This teaching, in addition to the endless hermeneutical question of its correct interpretation, raises a fundamental problem about situation ethics and moral consequentialism. It is not by chance that some authors, fascinated by this new moral teaching, have called for a "change of paradigm" in the moral sphere.

From here my discourse moves toward a philosophical and theological stance that seems to be common within the Church (though inadvertently): nominalism, i.e., the reduction of our theological words to a mere *flatus vocis*. For example, what is the right meaning of central concepts such as mercy, justice, pastoral care, and discernment? What do they mean today? The problem of nominalism is conducive to understanding Martin Luther's thoughts more clearly. After more than five hundred years since his revolutionary vision, his thoughts are still relevant and are intriguing to quite a few people within the Church.

Another central discourse in this book is the discussion about Vatican II. How should it be interpreted? Moreover, would correct hermeneutics be the solution to such a complicated issue? After more than sixty years, the Church is still divided about the correct interpretation of the last council. Vatican II claimed that ecumenism was something urgent and non-negotiable, which is true as long as the aim and the effort are to establish a visible unity of all Christians within the only Church of Christ. However, while the unity *ad extra* should still be pursued, the Church has discovered a disunity *ad intra*, never known before. What should we make of Vatican II then? It is neither a super-dogma nor a council to be ignored, but one of the twenty-one councils of the Church — no doubt the most problematic one. This question is the focus of one essay. There is also another essay on Vatican II, dedicated to the re-instatement of the permanent diaconate as discussed in the Council Aula, which examines requests, results, and problems.

From Vatican II the book moves to discuss some questions of moral theology. Firstly, the importance of *Humanæ Vitæ* and also some contemporary attempts to overcome it by linking *Amoris Laetitia* directly with *Gaudium et Spes*, thereby overlooking Paul VI's 1968 encyclical on marriage and life. One specific essay examines the uneasy path from the promulgation of *Gaudium et Spes* to *Humanæ Vitæ*, reviewing the theological and intra-ecclesial opposition in 1968. This vehement opposition to *Humanæ Vitæ*,

Introduction

together with the attempt to overcome it in the name of love and responsibility as envisaged by Vatican II's Constitution on the Church in the Contemporary World, is surely one cause of the unprecedented moral crisis in the Church. The collapse of moral theology has undoubtedly favoured the widespread moral crisis of sexual abuses and cover-ups within the Church.

A Marian essay completes this symphonic analysis of the truth. Perhaps it is something new to our reader: Our Lady's priesthood as a unique share in the only priesthood of Christ. I consider Mary as Immaculate Co-Redemptrix, who actively participated in our Redemption, offering in and with Christ to the Father the price of our salvation—that is, Jesus's most precious Blood and the maternal sorrow of Her Immaculate Heart. Our Lady holds a unique and indeed higher priesthood, a maternal one, in relation to the priests and to all the faithful.

The hope is that the reader himself might find the whole discourse symphonic and might enjoy listening to it. Despite the several instruments playing, the sheet music that I followed is singular—the music of Truth—trying to put it first and above all my ideas or convictions.

I

The Sacrament of Matrimony
AS THE SPOUSAL LOVE OF CHRIST FOR HIS CHURCH

MARRIAGE AS A COVENANT BETWEEN MAN AND WOMAN

To understand the profound meaning of the sacrament of matrimony, we will study it in light of God's covenant with his people, which is expressed as a spousal union between Yahweh and Israel (see Ez 16:8, 60; Is 62:5; Hos 2:21-22). God is the faithful bridegroom; Israel, loved and cherished above all others, is the bride, although not always faithful to this indissoluble love. The new Covenant, sealed in the Blood of Christ, is also presented as a betrothal: the marriage of the Lamb, whose bride is made of innumerable hosts of saints dressed in dazzling white linen (see Rev 19:7; 21:2; Eph 5:25). Here the bride of Christ is the triumphant Church that has welcomed, since her foundation on earth, all people of good will. This divine espousal is the *exemplar* and the inward sacramental *form* of the union between man and woman, in whom "the beginning" of God's creation (see Mt 19: 4-5) is recapitulated and remains open to a "love to the end" (see Jn 13:1) — the love of Our Lord who died for us on the Cross, perpetuating that sacrificial love in the Holy Eucharist, i.e., the gift of the Spouse to his Bride.[1]

Man and woman by the sacrament of matrimony are no longer two individual beings but "one flesh." The book of Genesis describes the joining of the two as a union in "one body," or more accurately, in "one flesh," which designates an intimate communion of life. Adam was not able to find a helpmate similar to him among any of the creatures made by God, except Eve, in whom he recognizes his own humanity and a "helper" of his

---

[1] For a broader view of the spousal meaning of the sacrifice of the Cross in relation to Jesus as the Bridegroom of the new covenant, and its relation to marriage as such, see B. Pitre, *Jesus as the Bridegroom: The Greatest Love Story Ever Told* (New York: Image, 2014).

own kind. As soon as he saw his wife he exclaimed: "This is at last bone of my bones and flesh of my flesh" (Gen 2:23). The union of the two is possible precisely through such a recognition. The text of Genesis then continues: "This is why a man leaves his father and mother and joins himself to his wife, and they become one flesh" (Gen 2:24).

THE PHRASE "ONE FLESH" POINTS TO THREE ELEMENTS:

> 1) the coming to be of a *new entity*, distinct from either of the constituent persons; 2) the fact that this entity is single, that is, not subject to recombination internally or externally; and 3) the fact that the entity is not an abstraction but an *organism*, enfleshed and endowed with life. Although the distinction is pre-philosophical and the narrative is not speculative or analytic in form, the maxim is proffered as a universal truth, detached from local, historical or even religious specificity, neither directed at a particular nation nor elicited from any nation's wisdom.[2]

The phrase "one flesh" reveals the very nature of the new entity created and sealed in the sacrament of marriage. With St. John Paul II, we conclude that the human body, by virtue of its visibility, is inscribed with the call to intimate communion and love. For John Paul II, the body has a "spousal meaning" and is a revelation of the person. In the account of man's creation (Gen 2:23-25), the human identity as revelation is discovered and affirmed when Adam, looking at his wife, says: "This is bone of my bones, and flesh of my flesh" (Gen 2:23). In this way, the human identity of both is announced,[3] and further, the meaning of the body, interiorly called to symbolize and realize the unity of man and woman, is enlightened. John Paul II writes:

---

[2] P. Mankowski, "Dominical Teaching on Divorce and Remarriage: The Biblical Date," in *Remaining in the Truth of Christ*, ed. R. Dodaro (San Francisco: Ignatius, 2014), 39.

[3] See John Paul II, General Audience (January 9, 1980), in *L'Osservatore Romano*, Weekly Edition in English (January 14, 1980), 1.

The Sacrament of Matrimony

The revelation, and at the same time the original discovery of the nuptial meaning of the body, consists in this: it presents man, male and female, in the whole reality and truth of his body and sex ('they were naked') and at the same time in full freedom from any constraint of the body and of sex. The nakedness of our progenitors, interiorly free from shame, seems to bear witness to this. It can be said that, created by Love, endowed in their being with masculinity and femininity, they are both 'naked' because they are free with the freedom of the gift. This freedom lies at the basis of the nuptial meaning of the body. The human body, with its sex, and its masculinity and femininity seen in the very mystery of creation, is not only a source of fruitfulness and procreation, as in the whole natural order. It includes right from the beginning the nuptial attribute, that is, *the capacity of expressing love, that love in which the person becomes a gift* and — by means of this gift — fulfils the meaning of his being and existence. Let us recall here the text of the last Council which declared that man is the only creature in the visible world that God willed 'for its own sake.' It then added that man 'can fully discover his true self only in a sincere giving of himself.'[4]

The sacrament of matrimony is rooted in God's creation and in the natural union of male and female, as evidenced from the beginning in the book of Genesis. Thus, when the Pharisees wonder about the legitimacy of divorce (see Mt 19:3-9; Mk 10:2-12), Jesus further establishes that man and woman build a new and perpetual bond in an indissoluble way of life. Jesus affirms the true concept of marriage by returning to the beginning: although Moses permitted divorce, "in the beginning it was not so" (Mt 19:8). In answering the objections of the Pharisees, Jesus connects Genesis 1:27 with Genesis 2:24. The new

---

4 John Paul II, General Audience, (January 16 1980), in *L'Osservatore Romano*, Weekly Edition in English, (January 21, 1980), 1.

entity made by "one flesh" now appears again in its sacramental fullness: "Have you not read that the Creator in the beginning made them male and female and that he said: This is why a man must leave father and mother, and cling to his wife, and the two become one body? They are no longer two, therefore, but one flesh. So then what God has united, man must not divide" (Mt 19:4-6).

St. Paul knows the teaching of the Lord and faithfully clings to it, showing its sacramental content by establishing a great analogy between the mystery of Christ and the Church and the mystery of matrimony. Through the apostle Paul in 1 Corinthians 7:10-11, the Lord himself commands that "a woman must not separate from her husband" and "a man must not divorce his wife." Matthew 19 is present here in the background.

Moreover, in 2 Corinthians 11:1-3 the discourse about marriage is brought to a higher level. Despite their infidelities, St. Paul suffered a divine jealousy for the community of the faithful in Corinth, for he arranged their marriage to Christ, presenting the whole body of believers to Him as a chaste virgin. The covenantal betrothal here receives a special light. The Corinthian Church is the chaste bride to marry this one husband or one man, Christ—in Latin, *"despondi enim vos uni viro virginem castam exibere Christo"* (2 Cor 11:2). At first, this discourse seems to ignore the relationship between male and female, and thus does not have a real reference to human marriage. However, if we read carefully, we find that the Pauline formula *one man* (*uni viro*), luminously echoes the classic *one flesh* or *one body* in reference to human marriage (Mt 19:16 and Gn 2:24). The sacramental unity of being one flesh is enlightened by a deeper unity: the presence of one man, Christ. Since Christ is one, reality is profoundly one on a metaphysical level, because it is shaped by Him. as proved by each entity created by God, in particular the reality of matrimony. *One man* and *one flesh* find their completion in the promise to realize a mystical betrothal between Christ and the Church, a chaste virgin. This espousal of unity reveals the perennial meaning of the truth about marriage.

This higher meaning of marriage is eventually and more explicitly depicted by St. Paul in his letter to the Ephesians

(5:29-32), in which he quotes the teaching of the Lord about marriage, echoing Genesis 2:23-24. This Pauline pericope speaks of a greater mystery than the human union of male and female. This is the "great analogy," as John Paul II has defined it. Urging Christian husbands to love their wives as their own bodies, St. Paul draws attention to a mystery which is the archetype of marriage — the love between Christ and the Church. He writes: "A man never hates his own body, but he feeds it and looks after it; and that is the way Christ treats the Church, because it is his body — and we are its living parts. *For this reason, a man must leave his father and mother and be joined to his wife, and the two will become one body.* This mystery has many implications; but I am saying it applies to Christ and the Church" (Eph 5:29-32, emphasis mine).

Marriage is a mystery clearly founded in the union of Christ and the Church. The love and communion of the one man with his bride is analogous to the union of man and woman who become one flesh by the nuptial meaning of their bodies. In other words, the man and woman become a sacramental participation of husband and wife in the indissoluble love of Christ for his Church through marriage. This great analogy is a share in the unique covenantal union with Yahweh, prefigured in the Old Testament by God's unique relationship with the people of Israel, and finally accomplished in Christ and his Church.

With all this in mind, we understand that matrimony is a sacrament of the New and Eternal Covenant.[5] While human marriage ends with the death of the spouses, the eternal matrimony of the Lamb and his Bride in the Blood of Christ is endless and introduces each sacramental marriage into this unending covenant with God. Divine grace given by Christ in the sacrament

---

5 Before the Council of Trent solemnly declared that marriage is a sacrament of the Evangelical Law that confers grace in order to condemn the errors of the protestant Reformers (see can. 1, sess. XXIV), the Council of Florence had declared already the following: "The seventh sacrament is matrimony, which is a figure of the union of Christ and the Church, according to the words of the apostle: 'This is a great sacrament, but I speak in Christ and in the Church'" (*Decree for the Armenians*).

of matrimony is drawn from the great mystery of which St. Paul speaks. Hence this sacrament realizes in a human couple that indissoluble love of Christ with His Church to the point of making the two into one—i.e., one new entity, a married couple embodying the one Mystical Body of Christ. We can thus unequivocally say that besides breaking a natural bond of unity, divorce contradicts this eternal covenantal love and communion.

With all this information in mind, we should be surprised to read the following in Pope Francis's recent encyclical on marriage and family, *Amoris Laetitia*:

> We should not however confuse different levels: there is no need to lay upon two limited persons the tremendous burden of having to reproduce perfectly the union existing between Christ and his Church, for marriage as a sign entails 'a dynamic process..., one which advances gradually with the progressive integration of the gifts of God.' (AL 122)

This statement requires immediate clarification. While it is true that a man and woman can never perfectly reproduce the mystery of unity between Christ and the Church, there will always be a void between human capacities and God's perfection. Nevertheless, this supernatural reproduction is granted by grace and not by human effort. The grace of matrimony *in mysterium* reproduces in human flesh that perfect supernatural union of Christ with his Church. The spouses are called to be faithful to that grace. Out of human weaknesses they can fail to bring this grace to fulfilment, but grace is never a "tremendous burden"; it is rather an easy yoke that sanctifies the family entity through the sacrament. Man and woman are not two solitary persons. Grace creates a beautiful reciprocal bond: the spouses' existence, sanctified by the sacrament, is already part of that greater union; conversely, the sanctifying union of Christ with his Church is manifested and lived out by the married couple in virtue of the sacramental mystery. The vivifying doctrine of the Church on marriage and divorce is like fresh bread to nourish our souls, never a heavy burden to weigh down men and women.

The Sacrament of Matrimony

THE ENEMIES OF MARRIAGE

Throughout the ages Christian marriage has always had enemies ready to undermine its meaning or even abolish is natural perpetuity. These enemies fought against its natural and sacramental bond of indissolubility. Why is indissoluble marriage feared? Indissolubility is linked with complementarity and therefore with a fontal covenantal union between God and man. It is a way to reach out to God, starting with the unity of reality, and in God we can see faith and reason, grace and nature profoundly united. Let us now examine the two capital enemies of marriage, the French Revolution and Martin Luther.

These two are actually interdependent since the Lutheran Revolution prepared the way for the French Revolution. The rejection of reason as an ally of faith had its practical consequence in the rejection of marriage as a perpetual bond between man and woman which symbolically expresses, as said above, the covenant between God and man. For example, Luther had already called into question the sacrament of matrimony, denying its sacramental character;[6] during the French Revolution marriage continued its decline with the formal introduction of a constitutional divorce.

Let us take a deeper look into Luther's understanding of matrimony, which seems to be influential in the Church today. His most important argument is laid out in his explanation of his Statements in 1521, in which he claims that matrimony cannot be a sacrament because it is not the mechanical working of the

---

[6] In his German work published at Wittenberg in 1530 under the title *Von den Ehesachen* (on Marriage), Luther writes: "No one indeed can deny that marriage is an external wordly thing, like clothes and food, house and home, subject to worldly authority, as shown by so many imperial laws governing it." In an earlier work, the original edition of *De Captivitate Babylonica* he declares more radically: "Not only is the sacramental character of matrimony without foundation in Scripture; but the very traditions, which claim such sacredness for it, are a mere jest." He also adds: "Marriage may therefore be a figure of Christ and the Church; it is however not a Divinely instituted sacrament, but the invention of men in the Church, arising from ignorance of the subject." A. Lehmkuhl, *Marriage* (Sacrament of), in *The Catholic Encyclopedia*, vol. IX (New York: Robert Appleton Company, 1910), 707.

sacrament but faith that brings salvation. The sacramental mode of effecting salvation *ex opere operato* would be a mechanical making of salvation, not salvation through faith. He says:

> From all this, I think it is clear that faith is necessary for the sacrament, a faith which does not doubt that it receives everything which the words declare and the sacraments signify... This saying, taken from the teachings of St. Augustine, holds true, "Not the sacrament but the faith in the sacrament makes righteous and saves."7

The penultimate argument in his view is derived from his understanding of marriage in the Bible. We do not read of a biblical promise of salvation anchored in marriage. Marriage according to Luther was not instituted by Christ, nor is it a sign of something deeper. Merely symbolic, matrimony can be a sort of allusion to Christ and the Church, but this symbolism can never effect a grace-filled marital bond flowing from the union between Christ and his Church. The fact that a sacrament cannot be an instrument of grace is a result of the fact that the Church cannot be an instrument of salvation. No mediation between Christ and the believer is possible except faith. Although Luther still maintains the Augustinian distinction between *signum* and *res* (the *action* expressed in sensible signs and the *grace*), from *The Babylonian Exile of the Church* (1520) onward he no longer applies it to marriage:

> We have said that in every sacrament there is a word of divine promise, to be believed by whoever receives the sign, and that the sign alone cannot be a sacrament. Nowhere do we read that the man who marries a wife receives any grace of God. There is not even a divinely instituted sign in marriage, nor do we read anywhere that marriage was instituted by God to be a sign of anything. To be sure, whatever takes place in a visible manner can be understood as a figure or allegory of

---

7 LW 32:17.

The Sacrament of Matrimony

something invisible. But figures or allegories are not sacraments, in the sense in which we use the term.[8]

As a result, marriage only has a place in the order of creation and not in the order of salvation. For the German Reformer, marriage is a bulwark against sin, but in no way is it a sanctifying means of grace. Marriage is an *ordinance of creation*.[9] As a man cannot be a woman and a woman cannot be a man, so too a man cannot live without a woman. Luther is also conscious that sin has corrupted human nature so that man is not always eager or even willing to respect God's law in creation. Sticking to his singular idea of human nature totally corrupted, Luther lays out two ways in which God governs the world: the spiritual and the worldly kingdoms. In the spiritual kingdom, the Holy Spirit leads Christians and righteous people under the Gospel of Christ. In the temporal, God restrains the non-Christians and the wicked in order to maintain an outward peace.[10] As there are two kingdoms in this world to rule over the people, so there are two laws of God regulating moral life.[11] One is spiritual, teaching righteousness under the influence of the Holy Spirit; the other is temporal or worldly, a law for those who cannot comply with the spiritual order. Luther applies this twofold moral vision to adultery, in reference to Matthew 5:32: Christians must not divorce, irrespective of adultery (spiritual law), but divorce exists and was granted by Moses (in the worldly law) because of sin. The permission of divorce should be seen as a limit that God places upon worldly people to contain their misbehavior and prevent them from worse actions, on the basis of their own maliciousness.[12]

Even though Luther has a positive, natural view of marriage, the fact that he denies its sacramental nature in Christ also poses problems for how he understands celibacy and virginity.

---

[8] LW 36:92.
[9] LW 1: Gen 2:23. Luther places marriage—on account of his exegesis of Gen 45:19—along with the fourth and the sixth Commandments. Therefore, the fundamental aim of marriage is to conceive children and raise them in the ways of God (LW 44:11-12).
[10] See LW 45:91.
[11] See LW 45:88-93.
[12] See LW 45:31.

Luther, in fact, opposes marriage to celibacy because only the latter is the "most religious state of all,"[13] and only it leads one to live spiritually.[14] Since all the faithful share in the common priesthood, there is no difference between ordinary folk and office-bearers in their spiritual relationship with God. Thus, if marriage is only a remedy to sin and is not related to grace as a sacramental means of sanctification, it can only be understood as an intermundane state of life that aims at de-clericalizing matrimony (as a result of its desacramentalization or perhaps as its logical conclusion). We've seen the consequences of Luther's view of divorce and adultery. Although it is disapproved of in the spiritual law, while being tolerated in the temporal law, divorce has become the custom of society. We know the consequences of divorce in our modern society: almost half of all marriages end in divorce, and thus, marriage is quickly disappearing from society. The a priori acceptance of a corrupted human nature (mainly out of a nominalist starting point) that we find in Luther was fatal indeed. It paved the way for our current society.

The Lutheran Reformation's rejection of reason as an indispensable aid to belief in God and its claim of "faith alone" in opposition to the sacrament led to a rejection of the sacrament of matrimony as an indissoluble bond. *Faith alone* is like a solitary man who casts doubt on the principle of one flesh as one perpetual bond. It began to stress the concept of the individual over that of man and family, where communion and alliance are necessary. The relationship between faith and reason is, in fact, a necessary prerequisite to any other possible union originating from the union between God and man in the Incarnation of Christ. While Luther rejected reason, the French revolutionaries rejected marriage as a perpetual union between one man and one woman. Strangely enough, the rejection of reason by Luther was echoed by an exaltation of *only reason* by French revolutionaries. However, in both cases the break of complementarity, either on account of faith or reason, provoked isolation and the rise of a freedom without reference to anything beyond itself.

---

13 LW 28:17. Here Luther comments on 1 Cor 7.
14 See LW 28:17.

These two enemies of marriage have their common roots in modern thought. Without doubt indissolubility can only be a scandal for those who theorize the absolute course of free will and the pre-eminence of the ego. In this context, indissolubility is slavery. After the Enlightenment, the essence of freedom was turned over from a personal capability of choosing in view of a good to a mere potentiality of thinking and acting in accordance with man's changeable desire. It is interesting to note that one of the first decisions made by the French National Assembly after the 1789 Revolution was a promulgation of a new law issued on September 20, 1792, according to which divorce was introduced in order to deliver an indissoluble marriage from ruin. For the revolutionaries, marriage was only a civil contract, whose dissolubility by divorce was a flag of man's freedom. From that time forward, this was the new manifesto of freedom: *marriage breaks up by divorce.*[15]

Before promoting divorce as a sign of free will, the Constituent of the French Revolution forbade any perpetual commitment, such as the professing of religious vows by nuns and friars: "The law does not recognize anymore either religious vows or any other engagement which is against natural right or the Constitution."[16]

THE SACRAMENT OF MATRIMONY ACCORDING TO THE LITURGICAL RITE

Marriage is a communion of love and society of life in a perpetual and indissoluble bond open to generating life. Liturgy is where the faith of the Church is manifested and becomes prayer and adoration of the mystery of God. In the liturgy of matrimony, we profess the faith about the sacrament of marriage founded on the rock that is the love of Christ for his Church, and in that act we are able to transform this faith and doctrine into a sublime prayer that sustains each marriage.

I would like to concentrate my attention now on the liturgy of matrimony in the *Vetus Ordo*, focusing on some features that highlight the mystery as we have received it directly from Our

---

15   See B. Dumont, "*Marriage Indissoluble et Modernité*," in *De Matrimonio*, ed. M. Ayuso (Madrid, 2015), 81-84.
16   Ibid., 83.

Lord and the New Testament. Liturgy has enriched the sacrament of matrimony with expressive rites, several of which have persisted from the earliest times of the Church. Some sacramentals, already in use in the pre-Christian era, have been accepted and sanctified by the Church, such as the veil, the ring, and the wreath. Pope Nicholas I (c. 866), in his answer to the Bulgars regarding the type of Christian marriage recognized in Rome, tells us that the whole ceremonial of a Christian matrimony is very simple and made up of two defined parts. First, we have the preliminaries that constitute the betrothal (*sponsalia*) in its broader sense. This ceremonial includes the expression of consent of the couple to be married, which constitutes the betrothal as such. This part is supplemented by 1) the *subarrahatio* — i.e., the delivery of the *arrhae* or pledges — represented ordinarily by the giving of a ring,[17] which Pope Nicholas I called the *annulus fidei*, the ring of fidelity; and 2) the handing over of the dowry, secured by a legal document in the presence of witnesses. The second part, which normally follows the *sponsalia*, is composed of 1) the celebration of the Holy Mass, 2) the solemn benediction of the spouses, and 3) the wearing of crowns as they leave the church.[18]

In the ceremony of betrothal, the ring in particular has a great symbology. According to Tertullian,[19] it is the sign of fidelity. For Clement of Alexandria, the ring is a seal showing that the wife is queen and mistress in the house. "He gives a gold ring," says Clement, "that she may with it seal up what has to be kept safe, as the care of keeping the house belongs to her."[20] The

---

17 The *subarrahatio* was already an institution of Roman Law received also by Germanic Law, and was part of the familiar tradition of the *sponsalia* together with the so called *dexterarum iunctio* and kiss. The ring testified to the delivery of a sum of money that in case of the dissolution of that marriage, the bridegroom would have lost or would have had the right to be given back, depending on who had broken the marriage.
18 H. Thurston, *Marriage* (Ritual of), in *The Catholic Encyclopedia*, 704.
19 Tertullian also speaks of the happiness of "that marriage which is made by the Church, confirmed by the Holy Sacrifice (*oblatio*), sealed by the blessing, which the angels proclaim and which is ratified by our Father in heaven." *Ad Uxores*, 2, 9. See Ibid.
20 *The Layfolk's Ritual* (London, 1916), 32.

The Sacrament of Matrimony

marriage ceremony embodies this particular and very expressive fact: it is only the husband who, after receiving the blessed and sprinkled ring from the priest, places it on the ring finger of the bride's left hand. This alludes to the theology of matrimony that we have seen in the teachings of St. Paul. As Christ is that one man to whom the Bride-Church is espoused, and as it is Christ who unites his Spouse to himself, so the bridegroom, symbolizing Christ, unites his bride to himself in a covenantal indissoluble love and marries her in Christ. By the imposition of a ring the power of the sacrament of matrimony is symbolized and a new union is effected by the power of grace, while the spouses exchange their vows of fidelity.

The priest underlines the fidelity of the bride for her bridegroom as the Church is faithful to Christ in the blessing of the ring:

> Bless thou O Lord this ring which we bless in thy name, that she who is to wear it may render to her husband unbroken fidelity. Let her abide in thy peace, and be obedient to thy will, and may they live together in constant mutual love.[21]

As the bridegroom places the ring on the bride's finger he says: "With this ring I thee wed, and I promise unto thee my fidelity."[22] The Church, united to Christ by the shedding of his precious Blood, is always the background of the whole rite of marriage. The meaning of the wife as a type of the Church, mysteriously united to Christ in virtue of his love and fidelity even unto death, is again perceptible in the nuptial blessing, which is given while the married couple kneel at the altar step:

> O God, by thy mighty power thou hast made all things out of nothing, and set in order the foundation of the universe. After which thou didst make man in thine own likeness, and appoint to him

---

[21] P. T. Weller, ed., *The Roman Ritual*, vol. I (New York: Boonville, 2007), 463.
[22] Ibid., 465.

woman to be his inseparable helpmate, in such wise that the woman's body had its beginning from the rib of the man, thereby teaching that what thou wast pleased to institute from one principle might never lawfully be put asunder. O God, thou hast created the marriage union, making it a sacrament so sublime that the nuptial bond has become an image of the mystical union of Christ with the Church. O God, by Whom woman is joined to man, on which fellowship society mainly depends and is endowed with the blessing which alone was never taken away, neither punishment for original sin nor by the sentence of the flood, mayest thou regard thy handmaid here present with bounteous kindness. For she is to be united to her husband in lifelong communion, and hence entreats thee for strength and protection.[23]

THE PRESENCE OF THE BLESSED VIRGIN MARY IN THE SACRAMENT OF MARRIAGE

Mary the Mother of God is an outstanding example of a holy wife and mother as well as a salvific aid, since Our Lady intercedes for us in Christ. The Lord has done great things in Our Lady. She is the mother of our Saviour and in him she is also our mother, the mother of the whole Church. Her life of union with St. Joseph in such a poor family environment at Nazareth testifies to her great virtue and self-gift. In relation to us, Our Lady shines uniquely as mother of the mystical Body of Christ. In conceiving and giving birth to Jesus by the work of the Holy Spirit, she became the Mother of God. On Calvary, faithfully staying at the foot of the Cross beside her Son, she re-generated in Christ the whole of mankind. We were born to eternal life through her; she is the mother of our new birth. She is the woman (see Jn 19:25-27) to whom Christ commends his beloved disciple, a representative of all the disciples of Christ. Mary is the woman who recapitulates the first woman, the first Eve. Therefore, Mary, on Calvary and throughout the life of

---

23   Ibid., 467–469.

The Sacrament of Matrimony

Christ, is the New Eve, who gives birth to us and prepares the maternal ministry of the Church. Our Lady precedes the Church and structures her inwardly, laying out for her a personal and an immaculate pattern of motherhood and virginity. The Holy Church, in being mother of all people generated to faith in Christ and to eternal life, imitates the Blessed Virgin Mary.

For this reason, we say that Mary is the "Virgin made Church" as St. Francis lovingly called her. Mary is the Church, both on Calvary and in her final stage of glory and glorification in Heaven, insofar as she was bodily assumed into eternal life. Mary represents the Church. In the words of St. Isidore of Seville (ca. 560–636), she is like a new earth, a virgin earth, from which Christ the Head and the Founder of the Church is born. The Church is born from the pierced side of Christ on the Cross. This gold thread that unites Mary, Christ, and Church becomes ever more visible when St. Isidore establishes a spousal parallel between Our Lady, who represents the Church, and Christ, who espouses his Bride. He says:

> Mary represents the Church, which, being wedded to Christ, conceived us as a virgin by the Holy Spirit and as a virgin bore us.[24]

Hence, if the Church is the Bride of Christ, and the sacrament of matrimony reflects and produces in the union of one flesh this bond of indissoluble love between Christ and his Church, Our Lady, who is the perfect Church, is also the true Bride of Christ. Consequently, she plays a particular role in every marriage. Marriage is a union of two persons. The mystical marriage of Christ, the Lamb of God, requires a partner who is both a person (as Christ is a person) and a mystical body. This partner is Mary the Spouse of Christ as New Eve and Co-Redemptrix — the one who co-jointly with Christ has brought about the salvation of mankind.

One of the first Fathers of the Church to call Mary "spouse of God" is St. Peter Chrysologus (ca. 380–ca. 450). Mary became

---

24 St. Isidore of Seville, *Allegorie* 139; PL 83,117, cit. from L. Gambero, *Mary and the Fathers of the Church: The Blessed Virgin Mary in Patristic Thoughts* (San Francisco: Ignatius, 1999), 376.

the spouse of Christ at the Annunciation. God sent his Angel, not to take the Virgin away from Joseph, but to give to her mystically to the true Spouse, Christ her Son. She belongs to Christ, and they together form one single body. As St. Peter Chrysologus puts it:

> The messenger flies swiftly to the spouse, in order to remove every attachment to a human marriage from God's spouse. He does not take the Virgin away from Joseph but simply restores her to Christ, to whom she had been promised when she was being formed in her mother's womb. Christ, then, takes his own bride; he does not steal someone else's. Nor does he cause any separation when he unites his own creature to himself, in a single body.[25]

A very ancient saying reads: *caro Christi caro Mariae* — the flesh of Christ is the flesh of Mary. Christ took his human nature from her and because of this profound unity she was able to take part uniquely in our Redemption. In the Incarnation, the joining of man and woman is perfectly fulfilled: Jesus and Mary are one flesh, *una caro*. They are mystically espoused in the sense that they accomplish our salvation together. Because of that, the sacrament of matrimony must reproduce this effect of the mystical and salvific love of Christ for his Mother and vice versa — their indissoluble and sacrificial love. Christ and Mary are the couple that gives a new matrimony the grace to be faithful to the end. The end is the supreme sacrifice of Golgotha (see Jn 13:1), which is eternal through its perpetuation in the mystery of the Holy Mass and Holy Eucharist. The Holy Eucharist is in fact a spousal love, the love of Christ for his Bride, Mary, and through Mary, the Church.

Jesus and Mary are perfectly bound in an eternal matrimony of love and self-donation, where love is not egoism but the gift of oneself. Every grace comes to a couple married in Christ from Jesus through Mary. Let us flee to Our Lady to ask her for the grace of giving fresh vigor to the Church by being faithful to

---

25 St. Peter Chrysologus, *Sermo* 140, 2; PL 52, 576. See Ibid., 297.

the perennial doctrine of Christ on marriage and family life. Divorce is not only a human break-up but a denial of love itself which is given in the sacrament as already perfected in Jesus and Mary. To all married people is given the task of being faithful to the grace of the sacrament, to the love of Jesus for Mary and the love of Mary for Jesus.

2

Amoris Laetitia:
THE JOY OF LOVE THAT DIVIDES THE CHURCH

AMORIS LAETITIA (AL) IS A POST-SYN-odal exhortation that Pope Francis offered to the whole Church on March 19, 2016. The exhortation, marked by Pope Francis's personal doctrine and pastoral vision regarding love in the family, summarizes two long years of synodal process.

The *sensus fidei* of the Church was shaken and confused in receiving this Exhortation. Although the document does not infallibly declare that those living in mortal sin following divorce and re-marriage can receive the Eucharist, it nevertheless causes dismay about various doctrinal points. Strong ambiguity reigns with the consequent possibility of interpreting the teaching of the Church in various subjective and hence conflicting ways, leaving moral judgment in a sort of uncertainty, according to individual cases. While the exhortation contains notable teachings explained with pastoral wisdom, a document must be judged in its entirety, not in parts.

I. A MAGISTERIUM FOR AL?

First, we must establish the degree of magisterial binding for this document. This document is undoubtedly of the authentic ordinary magisterium of the Roman Pontiff, at least according to the form of teaching. The question is whether it is a magisterial document *in toto* (regarding *res fidei et morum*), or only the Pontiff's pastoral contribution (perhaps even in this case *in toto*), or, in the final analysis, a magisterial document of a pastoral nature with a pastoral end (something somewhat new to the magisterium itself). Many commentators have addressed this question.

According to Cardinal Burke,[1] AL is in no way a magisterial

---

1 R. Burke, "*Amoris Laetitia* and the Constant Teaching and Practice of the Church," *National Catholic Register*, April 17, 2016, www.

document since the Pontiff says in n. 3 that "not all discussions of doctrinal, moral or pastoral issues need to be settled by interventions of the magisterium." However, immediately following this passage, the Pope continues: "Unity of teaching and practice is certainly necessary in the church, but this does not preclude various ways of interpreting some aspects of that teaching or drawing certain consequences from it." This second quote explains Pope Francis's intentions in AL: to interpret some aspects of the doctrine and the relative consequences, not necessarily with a (definitive) magisterial intervention. Pope Francis prefers taking little steps rather than teaching directly with his Petrine charism; consequently, the category *magisterium*, in his teaching, has a relatively broad meaning.[2]

Father Spadaro, one of the "official interpreters" of this pontificate, also comments on AL. In his judgment, AL is "an exhortation about love, not about the doctrine of marriage."[3] Therefore, it is not magisterial but pastoral. The exhortation "is not about the doctrine of marriage and the family. This is an important key for reading the document"[4] according to Spadaro, since "the whole document insists on a pastoral effort to ensure the growth of love."[5] We must not forget the subtitle of the Exhortation: "On Love in the Family."

Leaving aside the fact that Spadaro may have subjective ideas about the distinction between doctrinal and pastoral — in his own words, "the doctrine is *radically* pastoral"[6] — the doctrine

---

ncregister.com/daily-news/amoris-laetitia-and-the-constant-teaching-and-practice-of-the-church.
2   See also the interview released by Pope Francis in *La Nación*, December 7, 2014, at the point regarding "the disorientation of some." Here is the English translation: http:/www.lanacion.com.ar/1750350-pope-francis-god-has-bestowed-on-me-a-healthdose-of-unawareness.
3   A. Spadaro, *"Amoris Laetitia». Struttura e significato dell'Esortazione apostolica post-sinodale di Papa Francesco,"* in "La Civiltà Cattolica" II (2016) 109 (105-128). [Note: Translation ours.]
4   Ibid.
5   Ibid.
6   Interview of commentary on AL a few days after the promulgation, released by Vatican Radio, http://it.radiovaticana.va/news/2016/04/09/padre_spadaro_commenta_lesortazione_amoris_laetitia/1221566. Translation and emphasis ours.

immerses and transforms itself into ecclesial praxis. According to Spadaro's interpretation, the whole document examines, not the doctrine, but the practice of love. For, "if it is not possible to change an irregular situation, it is always possible to pursue this way of salvation,"[7] namely, the way of merciful love. Thus, while the praxis changes, the doctrine remains untouched. However, if "the Exhortation is an invitation to those who live in irregular situations to pursue a path of merciful love towards others,"[8] which leads to justifying an irregular situation, then the so-called pathway becomes the rule of action, eventually becoming a new doctrine, which will replace Our Lord's teaching on marriage. Jesus has not exhorted us to walk a pathway but has given us explicit norms to follow.

Mons. A. Livi offers the final commentary we will examine. According to Livi, because of the type of document and the arguments addressed, AL is a pontifical act of the third kind, namely a document which only gives pastoral guidelines. Thus, the exhortation is not an act of the magisterium, which teaches new doctrines or gives authoritative interpretations of dogma, but it only provides pastoral directions to bishops, clergy, and laity.[9]

Two points are essential: 1) the author of AL is the Pope (logically prescinding from the content of the teaching), not just the latest theologian; and 2) what he teaches is not always compatible with the magisterium of the Church. The teaching is new in many respects and does not agree with the doctrine of faith and morals on salient points. However, this does not necessarily mean that it is not magisterium and or that it is only the Pope's opinion, but rather that the Pope is teaching a doctrine susceptible to error. Let us take the word 'magisterium' in its obvious sense of authentic teaching (in this case, the Roman Pontiff's teaching) regarding faith and morals, at least — even if not always — insofar as they are treated *indirectly* since the

---

7 A. Spadaro, *"Amoris Laetitia: Struttura e significato,"* 109.
8 Ibid.
9 Ibid. A. Livi, Tante affermazioni che vanno chiarite, in «La Nuova Bussola Quotidiana» (April 13, 2016), www.lanuovabq.it/it/articoli-tante-affermazioni-che-vanno-chiarite-15849.htm.

exhortation intends to treat *directly* of love in the family. In fact, various passages in the document affirm a new principle in an almost apodictic manner.[10]

The fact that principles are formulated excludes the possibility that the Pope only wants to express an opinion. The document presents a personal view that is not always compliant with the magisterium, but this is not immediately perceptible

---

10   See AL 301: "Per questo non è più possibile dire..." AL 301: "I limiti non dipendono semplicemente da una eventuale ignoranza della norma." AL 52: "... le unioni di fatto o tra persone dello stesso sesso, per esempio, non si possono equiparare *semplicisticamente* al matrimonio." Emphasis ours. It is also significant that from paragraph 296 onwards the adjective *irregular*, attributed to situations, is always placed in inverted commas. Evidently, as confirmed by Card. Schönborn in the press conference presentation of AL, the intention of the document is to overcome the distinction between regular and irregular (see his whole speech at www.chiesa.espresso.repubblica.it/articolo/1351305). AL 139: "Ampiezza mentale, per non rinchiudersi con ossessione su poche idee, e flessibilità per poter modificare o completare le proprie opinioni." AL 297: "Si tratta di integrare tutti,... Nessuno può essere condannato per sempre, perché questa non è la logica del Vangelo!" This phrase is strongly ambiguous, because, if it intends to deny that the Church acknowledges and teaches that there is eternal damnation, it is against Revelation. AL 298 (the situations in which remarried divorcees find themselves): "non devono essere catalogate o rinchiuse in affermazioni troppo rigide senza lasciare spazio a un adeguato discernimento personale e pastorale". AL 304: "È meschino soffermarsi a considerare solo se l'agire di una persona risponda o meno a una legge o a una norma generale..." AL 305: "... un Pastore non può sentirsi soddisfatto solo applicando leggi morali a coloro che vivono in situazioni "irregolari", come se fossero pietre che si lanciano contro la vita delle persone." These expressions which are formulated as 'apodictic propositions' from which it is necessary to begin to think and act in a new manner, also prove that, although the exhortation distances itself from what is defined as a sort of obstinacy in doctrine and moral norms, disregarding the lives of people, it resorts all the same to theoretical principles which will then direct moral and pastoral action. It should be remembered throughout this article that the official English translation of AL generally seems to soften or even alter the meaning of the more controversial affirmations therein, as is the case for all the above quotations. When, in the passages we wish to quote, the English version is sufficiently distant from the original as to confuse the discourse, the Italian text will be given in the footnote.

to the reader, who takes what he reads *simpliciter* as the Pope's teaching. One cannot ask the faithful, or even the religious or the priest, to provide a hermeneutic of the text. This is not the reader's task. The reader should work to understand correctly, according to the immediate sense of the text, enlightened by the faith and reason.

The faithful are exposed to grave danger by receiving personal opinion as doctrine. De facto, the nature of the document and the mode of expression, especially in central points, present to the Church a post-synodal apostolic exhortation, of an equal value to *Familiaris Consortio, Reconciliatio et Paenitentia,* or *Sacramentum Veritatis.* Opinion or not, AL concerns the Church's doctrine on human love, marriage, and related sacraments, such as Holy Eucharist and confession. Although it does not comment on doctrine *ex professo*, it does emphasize the goal of providing a critical pastoral principle, which, in Francis's view, is *discernment* and help for people who live in irregular situations. Pastoral discernment is not a matter of reason alone but is based on dogmatic and moral doctrine. Thus, AL should be read, received, and critiqued according to the obvious, immediate sense of the words, particularly because most of the time and in the most delicate contexts, this sense remains obscure or ambiguous.

2. THE METHOD OF AL AS THE FOUNDATION OF THE HERMENEUTICAL QUESTION

The hermeneutical issue raised by the Apostolic Exhortation, because it is the background to all arguments, has become a capital issue, with the risk of obscuring all other questions. The hermeneutical question of AL arises from a fundamental fact: the Apostolic Exhortation *Familiaris Consortio* n. 84 was not cited once. By quoting only sections of the teaching on the necessity of the discernment of situations and excluding the substantial and definitional part, Francis seems to pave the way for a new sacramental praxis, prescinding the Scriptural teaching that does not admit remarried divorcees to Eucharistic Communion. It 'seems' so, since it is not said explicitly. Yet, AL's entire approach—and above all the controversial points of chapter VIII—reveals a proposal that distances itself from the magisterium hitherto expressed. The omitted part of *Familiaris Consortio* n. 84, so central—after all—for AL, says:

> However, the Church reaffirms her practice, which is based upon Sacred Scripture, of not admitting to Eucharistic Communion divorced persons who have remarried. They are unable to be admitted thereto from the fact that their state and condition of life objectively contradict that union of love between Christ and the Church which is signified and effected by the Eucharist. Besides this, there is another special pastoral reason: if these people were admitted to the Eucharist, the faithful would be led into error and confusion regarding the Church's teaching about the indissolubility of marriage.
>
> Reconciliation in the sacrament of Penance which would open the way to the Eucharist, can only be granted to those who, repenting of having broken the sign of the Covenant and of fidelity to Christ, are sincerely ready to undertake a way of life that is no longer in contradiction to the indissolubility of marriage. This means, in practice, that when, for serious reasons, such as for example the children's upbringing, a man and a woman cannot satisfy the obligation to separate, they 'take on themselves the duty to live in complete continence, that is, by abstinence from the acts proper to married couples.'[11]

The hermeneutical question is born here. Pope John Paul II is clear about the situation of the divorced and remarried: only those who repent, receive the sacrament of Confession, and then live in abstinence can be readmitted to Holy Communion. In the case of AL, which seems to obfuscate the issue, can Francis actually deviate from a praxis enlightened by the magisterium and founded on Sacred Scripture? He certainly cannot. Then

---

11   John Paul II, *Post-Synodal Apostolic Exhortation Familiaris Consortio*, November 22, 1981, in AAS 74 (1982) 185-186.

why does Francis do it, at least implicitly, by passing over the previous teaching in silence and broadening the subject to include multiple, variegated interpretations according to the cultural and national context, with a new theology—not always correct—serving as a background?

AL itself poses the problem, namely the question of interpretation; it supports the most diverse and even contradictory interpretations, for everyone can play interpreter to a document that is so ambiguous. Every hermeneutic could be the correct one, after all. One might be tempted to invoke Benedict XVI's principle for the correct interpretation of the Second Vatican Council, namely, "reform in the continuity of the one subject-Church," seeking, with all possible effort, to interpret AL in light of the Church's tradition. Strong in the knowledge that AL never denies previous doctrine and praxis, one could read it—similar to Vatican II—in continuity. Nevertheless, this approach is not only hazardous, but also impossible. AL does not change (*ipso facto*) the Church's praxis concerning irregular unions. Yet, the fact that the praxis and—behind it—the doctrine do not change does not ensure that the document is in continuity with the doctrines of the Church. In truth it is not, for one is explicitly invited "[not to] disregard the constructive elements in those situations[12] which do not yet or no longer correspond to her [the Church's] teaching on marriage" (AL 292).[13] Is this a move toward the gradualness of the law, in which the "constructive elements" ultimately lead to evaluating the entire situation under a new light, deviating from the law—both natural and canonical—regarding marriage? If the "constructive elements" are evaluated in an essential manner, changing the situation due to circumstances,[14] could a parish priest admit remarried divorcees to Communion? The growing trend, without the smallest sign

---

12   The Italian text of AL says it more explicitly and in a positive manner: "valorizzare gli elementi costruttivi in quelle situazioni."
13   Here the Pope takes up the thought of the Synod Fathers and makes it his own.
14   As we say further on, the elements are accidentals like the circumstances with respect to the substance which is the living *more uxorio*. The accidents never change the substance but only determine it.

of clarification from the Holy See, indicates that the answer is in the affirmative.

The greater problem is not the conclusion drawn but the premises which support it. Moreover, it is necessary to look beyond the *hic et nunc* of the exhortation to its long-term effect, which will be the reconfiguring of moral doctrine, starting from the new principles laid down in the exhortation. The praxis under consideration will change, but so will the perception of moral theology and, therefore, its pastoral application, beginning, for example, with "It can no longer [...] be said..." (AL 301).[15] Let us recall the words of Mons. Schneider, who said that it is:

> realistically insufficient to affirm that AL would be interpreted according to the traditional doctrine and practice of the Church. When in an ecclesiastical document, which in our case is devoid of a definitive and infallible character, elements of interpretations and applications are discovered which could have dangerous spiritual consequences, all the members of the Church, and in the first place the bishops — as fraternal collaborators of the Sovereign Pontiff in the effective collegiality — have the right to indicate respectfully this fact and to ask for an authentic interpretation.[16]

---

15   The Argentine Bishop Fernandez, a close collaborator of Francis (probably in the drafting of AL), has confirmed in one of his interviews that the whole chapter VIII, which is not even the most important one (the most important chapters would be IV and V), must not be reduced to the question of remarried divorcees. It aims rather to "open new doors both for moral and pastoral theology, which become more merciful, more transformed by the primacy of charity and closer to people's concrete reality." M. Fernandez, *Il popolo di Dio ha accolto bene Amoris laetitia*, interview of June 13, 2016, http://www.lastampa.it/2016/06/13/vaticaninsider/ita/inchieste-e-interviste/fernandez-il-popolo-di-dio-ha-accolto-bene-amoris-laetitia-oh8mOmKVDedrUO-JNIie9AL/pagina.html [Translation ours.]

16   A. Schneider, *"Amoris laetitia": a need for clarification in order to avoid a general confusion*, April 24, 2016, http://voiceofthefamily.com/official-english-translation-of-bishop-schneiders-reflection-on-amoris-laetitia/

AL lays down a kind of permanent hermeneutic or process of indefinite hermeneutics that begins not from the need to clarify something—the praxis until now was clear—but from the hope of reaching a more enlightened discernment. Thus, the hermeneutic is, in a manner, established as the science necessary for receiving the Pope's teaching. If the Pope, supreme pastor and doctor of the nations, asks the faithful and priests to provide a hermeneutic suited to his words, who will reconcile or judge the differing, even contrasting and contradictory, hermeneutics? We have gone beyond the problem of interpreting the Second Vatican Council to interpretating the Pope. If even the Pope must be interpreted, who will be the official and authorized interpreter of the faith in the Church? Will Francis's synodal decentralisation (of which we have yet to see much evidence!) lead to a dissolution of the unity of faith and morals? Case by case becomes nation by nation (cf. AL n. 3), a problem which does not yet exist, but which amounts to that careless openness to modernity taken as *unicum* and not critically analysed on its various levels. The hermeneutical necessity, a problem of continuous and involved interpretation, is but one effect of this unconditional and acritical openness.

3. THE THEOLOGICAL APPROACH OF AL

The exhortation "on love in the family" favors a more anthropological approach, rather than theological *stricto sensu*. It first discusses the relationship of man to God, then the historical family with its problems and weaknesses, and finally, grace and the sacraments. At the heart of it lies the concrete family, not abstract theological ideals (cf. AL 36-37). For this reason, perfection is treated as something of an ideal and is deferred to eternal life. Here, in this life, one must face concrete situations and cope with the problems of life without judging anyone. According to Francis, "no family drops down from heaven perfectly formed; families need constantly to grow and mature in the ability to love" (AL 325). Therefore,

> [o]ur contemplation of the fulfilment which we have yet to attain also allows us to see in proper

perspective the historical journey which we make as families, and in this way to stop demanding of our interpersonal relationships a perfection,[17] a purity of intentions and a consistency which we will only encounter in the Kingdom to come. It also keeps us from judging harshly those who live in situations of frailty. (Idem)

The emphasis is on the historical and social existence of the family, rather than the sacrament of marriage, which actually bestows the grace to be faithful to one's promises in this life. By making existence the starting point, perfection is deferred to the definitive Kingdom, while we must make do with fragility and imperfection for the present moment. The acceptance of self, as concrete and historical subjects, takes precedence over being a new creation through grace.

The particular teaching of AL on becoming what Christ is for the Church through the sacrament of marriage, and vice versa, leaves us somewhat perplexed:

> We should not however confuse different levels: there is no need to lay upon two limited persons the tremendous burden of having to reproduce perfectly the union existing between Christ and his Church, for marriage as a sign entails 'a dynamic process..., one which advances gradually with the progressive integration of the gifts of God.' (AL 122)

As the Pope says, spouses will not be able to reproduce "perfectly" the union between Christ and his Church, but they will be able to so in the measure in which they cooperate with God. This is not a tremendous burden, but it is a sweet yoke, a gift of sacramental grace, in union with sanctifying grace. The reproduction of the spousal union of Christ with the Church is a gift of grace and, as Pope Francis says, it is essential to cultivate, above all, trust in this grace (see AL 36). Nevertheless, in the

---

17 Compare to the Italian text, "per smettere di pretendere dalle relazioni interpersonali una perfezione."

Christian tradition, we find a slightly different interpretation of Ephesians 5:21-33. The sacrament of marriage, *in mysterium*, already reproduces in human flesh the perfect supernatural union between Christ and the Church, to which the spouses are called to configure themselves. Man and woman are not two solitary beings. Grace creates a mysterious reciprocal bond; the existence of the spouses, sanctified by the sacrament, is already part of that "great mystery" (Eph 5:32) of which St. Paul speaks, while the sanctifying union of Christ and his Spouse-Church is shown in and lived by married couples through grace. As John Paul II so aptly describes in *Familiaris Consortio*, "Family, become what you are" (n. 17). In other words, the marriage is *already* a sign of Christ's love for His Church, and the husband and wife must continually strive to live that image through their everyday lives, in the midst of their struggles, difficulties, and joys.

There is another reason to underline the singularity of this document. Francis begins the document by talking about the world, and then moves to discuss God in the context of the family. Is he making a personal, papal theological choice by beginning this way, or does this imply a desired change of perspective in all magisterial teaching? The recent and constant pontifical magisterium has always preferred the other way: from God to man, from Revelation to humankind. This is the way of the mystery of the Incarnation.

One of the Pope's guiding criterions shows that he views history as a journey in time rather than a reason to become "static" in space: " ... time is greater than space" (AL 3). The Pontiff explains this premise, saying that "it is more important to start processes than to dominate spaces" (AL 261).[18] More than fixity

---

18 A more exhaustive explanation of this premise is found in *Evangelii Gaudium* 222: AAS 105 (2013) 1111. Pope Francis's theologian, Bishop Fernandez, explains this premise in a still more simple and direct manner, almost as though there were an inertial force in the application of the things of faith and morals: "Time will put things in their place, and the Pope understands it thus: 'time is superior to space'. Some changes make too much noise but then everything settles." M. Fernandez, *Il popolo di Dio ha accolto bene Amoris laetitia*, cit. [Translation ours.]

in a place, the historical process is about *becoming*. Therefore, in the theological sense of this phrase, the the *experience* of grace becomes the focal point. If experience grows in time, then the journey will take priority over the grace. The Pope is not claiming that man can forego grace. However, without the *becoming* aspect, there would not even be an experience of grace, which is given in as much as historically existing man draws near to it and grabs a piece of it (see AL 297). AL rejects the philosophical proposition that being is followed by becoming. The journey comes first and then the grace, entirely relative to the time into which it crosses. In the words of Francis:

> [i]t is reductive simply to consider whether or not an individual's actions correspond[19] to a general law or rule, because that is not enough to discern and ensure full fidelity to God in the concrete life of a human being. (AL 304)

The discernment, then,

> is dynamic; it must remain ever open to new stages of growth and to new decisions which can enable the ideal to be more fully realized. (AL 303)

4. THE PRINCIPAL CONTENTS OF AL

The previous considerations lead us to the exhortation's moral doctrine about divorcees who have entered into a new union *more uxorio (as husband and wife)*. Francis offers an approach characterized by understanding and mercy. Unfortunately, this approach often leads to a subjectivist view of how mercy is shown to an individual, both by God and by the Church. Thus, the gravest interpretation risk of chapter VIII relative to "accompanying, discerning and integrating weakness," is promoting de facto (even without willing per se) a *situation ethics*.[20] The

---

19 The original text has a stronger meaning: "è meschino soffermarsi a considerare solo se l'agire di una persona risponda o meno [...]."
20 Situation Ethics is defined as follows by Pius XII: "Le signe distinctif de cette morale est qu'elle ne se base point en effet sur les lois morales universelles, comme par exemple les Dix Commandements,

various circumstances in which remarried divorcees find themselves could lead to mitigating the subjective judgment on their state, and then the objective one. Finally, this interpretation would consist of the de facto acceptance of irregular situations, which would eventually become regular. The adjective *irregular* is marked by quotation marks from n. 296 onwards, clarifying the intended sense.

AL introduces the need to discern the various situations that could arise:

> The divorced who have entered a new union, for example, can find themselves in a variety of situations, which should not be pigeonholed or fit into overly

mais sur les conditions ou circonstances réelles et concrètes dans lesquelles on doit agir, et selon lesquelles la conscience individuelle a à juger et à choisir. Cet état de choses est action humaine. C'est pourquoi la décision de la conscience, affirment les tenants de cette éthique, ne peut être commandée par les idées, les principes et les lois universelles. La foi chrétienne base ses exigences morales sur la connaissance des vérités essentielles et de leurs relations ; ainsi fait S. Paul dans l'Epitre aux Romains 3 pour la religion comme telle, soit chrétienne, soit anté-rieure au christianisme : à partir de la création, dit l'Apôtre, l'homme entrevoit et saisit en quelque sorte le Créateur, sa puissance éternelle et sa divinité, et cela avec une telle évidence qu'il se sait et se sent obligé à reconnaître Dieu et à lui rendre un culte, de sorte que négliger ce culte ou le pervertir dans l'idolâtrie est gravement coupable, pour tous et dans tous les temps. Ce n'est point ce que dit l'éthique dont Nous parlons. Elle ne nie pas, sans plus, les concepts et les principes moraux généraux (bien que parfois elle s'approche fort d'une semblable négation), mais elle les déplace du centre vers l'extrême périphérie. Il peut arriver que souvent la décision de la conscience leur corresponde. Mais ils ne sont pas, pour ainsi dire, une collection de prémisses, desquelles la conscience tire les conséquences logiques dans le cas particulier, le cas d'«une fois». Non pas! Au centre se trouve le bien, qu'il faut actuer ou conserver, en sa valeur réelle et individuelle; par exemple, dans le domaine de la foi, le rapport personnel qui nous lie à Dieu." *Ad Delegatas Conventui internationali Sodalitatis vulgo nuncupatae «Fédération Mondiale des Jeunesses Féminines Catholiques»*, in AAS 44 (1952) 414-415 (413-419). See also Pius XII on the same topic in his *Nuntius radiophonicus de conscientia christiana in iuvenibus recte efformanda*, in AAS 44 (1952) 270-278 and Instructio Suprema Sacra Congregatio S. Ufficii, *De Ethica Situationis*, in AAS 48 (1956) 144-145.

rigid classifications leaving no room for a suitable personal and pastoral discernment. (AL 298)[21]

The document then discusses the "mitigating circumstances in pastoral discernment," starting from the fact that "the Church possesses a solid body of reflection concerning mitigating factors and situations" (AL 301). This consideration gives rise to a new moral principle, an apodictic proposition that can easily become the guiding light for the pastoral action of discernment:

> Hence it is [sic] can no longer simply be said that all those in any 'irregular' situation[22] are living in a state of mortal sin and are deprived of sanctifying grace. More is involved here than mere ignorance of the rule. A subject may know full well the rule, yet have great difficulty in understanding "its inherent values", or be in a concrete situation which does not allow him or her to act differently and decide otherwise

---

21   This paragraph contains the debated note 329, in which the Pontiff mentions that "many" who, if they live as "brother and sister" in these irregular situations, would put their fidelity in question and compromise the good of the children. As support, the document cites *Gaudium et Spes* 51 of Vatican II, which ironically refers to *married couples* who find they are unable to have more children for a certain period. Hence, they are confronted with the difficulties which can take over in their married life. Many have attempted to explain what the Pope meant in this footnote with its accompanying citation. The fact that "expressions of intimacy" are referred to and not "conjugal acts" or "conjugal intimacy," as the Council says, would be the correct interpretation to demonstrate that the Pope does not equate these unions with marriage. In any case, the terminology "expressions of intimacy," which is not immediately comparable with conjugal intimacy or conjugal acts, tells us that, according to its immediate sense, a union *more uxorio* would be justifiable as such and that fornication in many of these situations would not be a sin. Interpreting this note, as Father Angelo Bellon does commendably, in the perspective of *Humanæ Vitæ* — to avert a possible heresy — is an exercise for theologians. See Fr. Bellon's article at http://chiesa.espresso.repubblica.it/articolo/1351288?eng=y.

22   By the omission and addition of words, the meaning is significantly altered from the original: "Per questo non è più possibile dire che tutti coloro che si trovano in qualche situazione cosiddetta 'irregolare' [...]."

without further sin. As the Synod Fathers put it,[23] "factors may exist which limit the ability to make a decision." (AL 298)

The "non è più possibile dire (it is no longer possible to say)" establishes a new process, which is not reflected either in defined doctrine or ordinary magisterium. These words indicate a general norm that opposes the reality of the person, drastically and universally separating the person from his actions and concrete choices. In truth and as Karol Wojtyła demonstrates in his Thomistic personalism philosophy, acts are not added to an existing subject; rather, a person is one with his acts. He grows in greatness or wretchedness through his moral choices. A person making one of the most important choices of his life — who marries, or decides to cohabit, or chooses to establish a new union after a divorce — is not merely changing his status from *single*. His new *status vitae* will intimately shape his existence, because such an action has profound moral consequences. His life is perfected or impoverished because of his good or bad moral choice. The danger is that the case becomes a norm, and the norm, in its turn, is applied in more subjective cases. AL carefully avoids the old casuistry of morality and opens an almost unlimited classification of possible cases.

However, one who lives in an objectively immoral situation, such as adultery and fornication, is also subjectively culpable, unless he is not responsible for that choice — thus, falling outside the moral sphere — due to lack of full awareness or undeliberate consent. According to *Veritatis Splendor* 52,[24] when no circumstance can dispense from the negative precepts of natural law,

---

23 Compare the English version to the original: "Come si sono bene espressi i Padri sinodali [...]."
24 "The *negative precepts* of the natural law are universally valid. They oblige each and every individual, always and in every circumstance. It is composed of prohibitions which forbid a given action *semper et pro semper*, without exception, because this kind of behavior is never compatible with the goodness of the will of the acting person, with his vocation to life with God and to communion with his neighbor. It is prohibited — to everyone and in every case — to violate these precepts. They oblige everyone, regardless of the cost, never to offend in anyone, beginning with oneself, the personal dignity common to all." in AAS 85 (1993) 1175.

the sixth commandment is binding *semper et pro semper*. Adultery and fornication are not less culpable or more acceptable by reason of the circumstances surrounding those acts, except in cases or invincible ignorance or deprivation of liberty. Can one usually say that those cohabitating *more uxorio* are invincibly ignorant about the divine-natural law and the ecclesiastical law, which forbid divorce and adultery without exceptions? Do they often find themselves so involved due to an absence of deliberate consent? Certainly not. The "non è più possibile dire" cannot be said and has never been said before.

AL denies *a priori* that inculpably living *more uxorio* could derive from an ignorance of the rule (cf. AL 301). It also reiterates the idea about mitigating circumstances:

> because of forms of conditioning and mitigating factors, it is possible that in an objective situation of sin—which may not be subjectively culpable, or fully such—a person can be living in God's grace, can love and can also grow in the life of grace and charity, while receiving the Church's help to this end" ["In certain cases, this can include the help of the sacraments", note 351]. (AL 305)

The factors mitigating moral responsibility, first listed in the *Catechism of the Catholic Church* (nn. 1735. 2352, cit. in AL 302), all refer to a wound inflicted either to the intellect, through ignorance and inadvertence, or to the will, through fear, habit, inordinate affections, and other psychological or social factors. AL 308 adds other mitigating circumstances, described only as "psychological, historical and also biological." It is difficult to evaluate the extension and the meaning of historical and biological mitigating circumstances. Social circumstances also have a broad definition. If one affirms these new factors as complementary to those in the *CCC*, the more religious LGBT groups could use this broader definition to justify homosexuality and gender theory, as an example.

The circumstances that mitigate subjective responsibility due to lack of full awareness or free consent never transform an objective disorder into a good, or sin into grace. To admit people living in irregular situations to the sacraments of confession and Eucharist, they must resolve to live as "brother and sister." It is the only way to ensure that the two, though living in an objectively immoral situation, are subjectively free from sin and can live in the grace of God. They are still obligated to avoid scandal since the union of two people affects the public sphere and is never a private affair.

If one wants to act outside the praxis because it is too rigid, then he must submit to the subjective justification of the objective moral disorder. Such is the whole effort of AL *a fortiori* in the development of chapter VIII. In the internal forum, a priest can never leave someone who desires the sacraments in ignorance or a condition of subjective irresponsibility, given the cogency of God's commandment against divorce and adultery. Further, because of the *public* character of marriage or a *more uxorio* union, the mitigating circumstances, while they can be subjective, will never be objective.

AL does not account for the public element of marriage or extramarital unions ("irregular situations"). Recognition of the public aspect implies that only marriage belongs wholly to the sphere of the common good and that an illegitimate union damages it. Nevertheless, if we follow the guidelines of AL, pastoral discernment could even consider — in certain cases — admitting remarried divorcees, who have not committed to living as brother and sister, to the sacraments. That practice provokes a breach in the public sphere and ends by privatizing it, that is, by reducing the public to the private. Regrettably, AL reduces *more uxorio* unions to the private sphere (case by case, as a rule) and consequently, reduced marriage as well.

Our culture tends to privatise everything, but especially marriage and family. When the family is reduced to the sphere of individual goods, other unions, like the homosexual one, boast the desire to become "family" at all costs, with the relevant equal rights and duties, even though this objectively can never be possible. AL does not provide a solution to this radical contradiction. The family is privatised, and homosexual love, which only concerns the affective sphere of two people, is made public. The evaluation of situations on a case by case basis could eventually overturn the Church's current praxis, which is founded on Sacred Scripture and Tradition. Worse still, individualistic and situation ethics may lead to the privatisation of the family. The family will no longer be viewed as a universal and common good, but a good for a few, the effect of an accentuated casuistry which must accommodate all possible situations in which remarried divorcees who are separated from their families can find themselves. The family will be separated from human life.

Let us turn our attention to AL's scriptural exegesis (nn. 185–186) on 1 Corinthians 11:17-34. Various commentaries on the text have said little, if anything, on the subject. Yet, it is an essential point of the Exhortation that seems to prepare the exegetical possibility for everyone to approach the Eucharist. According to AL, the "immediate and direct" meaning of the Pauline text is "markedly social" (AL 185):

> The wealthier members tended to discriminate against the poorer ones, and this carried over even to the *agape* meal that accompanied the celebration of the Eucharist. While the rich enjoyed their food, the poor looked on and went hungry: 'One is hungry and another is drunk. Do you not have houses to eat and drink in? Or do you despise the Church of God and humiliate those who have nothing?' (vv. 21–22). (AL 185)

Although some divisions existed in the Corinthian community during the Eucharistic celebration preceded by the *agape* or convivial meal, this does not mean that the divisions were essentially social nature, i.e., discrimination against the poor who did not have much to eat. Instead, Paul tells us that the abuses focused on the eating and drinking itself, transforming that Eucharistic assembly into a party where the poor were discriminated against and the real reason for congregating—to offer the Body and Blood of Christ—was forgotten. AL does not quote Paul's admonition: "Therefore whosoever shall eat this bread, or drink the chalice of the Lord unworthily, shall be guilty of the body and of the blood of the Lord. [...] For he that eateth and drinketh unworthily, eateth and drinketh judgment to himself, not discerning the body of the Lord."

This pericope focuses on worthily approaching the Body and Blood of the Lord. One ought to *recognize* what he is doing; he should not simply eat bread or drink wine whilst excluding some from partaking, thereby contradicting the very meaning of the Eucharist, the "sacrifice of thanksgiving." The successive liturgical tradition has eliminated the fraternal meal from the celebration of Holy Mass to prevent anyone from falling into such abuses and to ensure that all the faithful, whether poor or rich, might concentrate on the offering of the holy sacrifice, partaking in holy communion whilst living in union with the Lord and not as his enemies in sin. AL draws a singular conclusion from its social interpretation of the Pauline pericope:

> The Eucharist demands that we be members of the one body of the Church.[25] [...] When those who receive it turn a blind eye to the poor and suffering, or consent to various forms of division, contempt and inequality, the Eucharist is received unworthily. (AL 186)

The unworthiness, in this instance, is a result of not being in God's grace, i.e., a violation of God's commandments, particularly love of neighbor; it does not only come from social requirements. Since the text implies that the poor should integrate, 'poor' meaning those who live in difficult and irregular moral situations, thus alluding more to a moral than a material poverty, then one cannot pass over the insinuation in silence. Who are the discriminated and poor in the Church today? Does the category include the civilly remarried divorcees? According to AL, this fundamentally

---

25 The vocabulary is of *integration* in the original: "L'Eucaristia esige l'integrazione nell'unico corpo ecclesiale." Before the sentence given above, our author quotes a sentence which is entirely absent from the English version of AL: "Questo testo biblico è un serio avvertimento per le famiglie che si rinchiudono nella loro propria comodità e si isolano, ma più specificamente per le famiglie che restano indifferenti davanti alle sofferenze delle famiglie povere e più bisognose."

inclusive vision, beyond a mere social requirement, is "pastoral discernment filled with merciful love, which is ever ready to understand, forgive, accompany, hope, and above all integrate" (AL 312), instead of "a cold bureaucratic morality" (Idem). More clearly, "[i]t is a matter of reaching out[26] to everyone, of needing to help each person find his or her proper way of participating in the ecclesial community and thus to experience being touched by an 'unmerited, unconditional and gratuitous' mercy" (AL 297). Moreover, for the baptized who are divorced and civilly remarried, "[t]he logic of integration is the key to their pastoral care, a care which would allow them not only to realize that they belong to the Church as the body of Christ, but also to know that they can have a joyful and fruitful experience in it" (AL 299).

Who then are the poor in Western society? Questions such as these arise and hermeneutics which multiply because the text is not clear but leaves the reader to draw his own conclusions.

Surprisingly, the exhortation never cites or comments on the gospel texts containing the *ipsissima verba Christi* that teach the truth about marriage, explicitly condemning divorce and adultery.[27] Divorce is treated as a dispute that contextualizes Jesus' teaching on marriage:

> [It is] the presence of pain, evil and violence that break up families and their communion of life and love. For good reason Christ's teaching on marriage (cf. Mt 19:3–9) is inserted within a dispute about divorce.[28]

---

26 The English version here is drastically different from the original Italian: "si tratta di integrare tutti".

27 Mt 19:3–9 and 5:31–32; Mk 10:2–12; Lk 16:18 in line with I Cor 7:10–11: "But to them that are married, not I but the Lord commandeth. . . ." Unlike an apostolic counsel regarding continence for the unmarried and the widows (vv. 8-9), here Paul diligently clarifies that marriage as one and indissoluble is a divine precept and that what he teaches he has received from the Lord (as for the Eucharist, see I Cor 11:23–26).

28 AL 19 is the only time the text of Mt 19:3–9 is cited. AL 62 makes reference to the indissolubility of marriage according to the words of the Lord. The lemma "adultery" is not mentioned once, while it is dismaying that "erotismo più sano" is spoken of (AL 151) which must not be despised or neglected (see AL 157).

CONCLUSION

We offer these reflections with the sole intention of seeking the truth. They are given according to same perspective as AL and Pope Francis, who has not only reminded us during the Synods on the Family to speak with *parrhesia*, but has also explained (as in AL 2) that the synodal journey opened discussions for the family's situation in today's world. Because of the complexity of these issues, he has declared the need "for continued open discussion of a number of doctrinal, moral, spiritual, and pastoral questions."

Given this synodal freedom and *parrhesia*, the Pontiff asks pastors and theologians to contribute in arriving at greater clarity, which — as we have seen — is lacking in the magisterial document. As the Pope says, "The thinking of pastors and theologians, if faithful to the Church, honest, realistic and creative, will help us to achieve greater clarity." (Idem) This goal — to contribute to this investigation and clarification, ready to correct or retract whatever in our writing is not compliant with the faith of the Church — is close to our heart.

AL should be received critically, not passively, perceiving a kind of *super-magisterium* since the Pope is the author. On the other hand, it should not be discounted, given the numerous points of doctrine and of pastoral approach explained simply and directly, as is characteristic of Pope Francis. However, in salient points and central passages, the document proves unclear and ambiguous, vulnerable to many and contrasting hermeneutics. The points we have discussed need to be clarified by the magisterium of the Church.

The exhortation exposes another risk, beyond the passages that sound ambiguous to common sense and intellect enlightened by faith. It introduces a radical new magisterial approach to the facts of the faith by favoring a theological method that is cherished by certain modern theologians but always criticised by the magisterium. The bottom-up method, from man "in flesh and bones" — as Feuerbach would say — to God starts from experience and contingency to draw towards the mystery. This approach emphasizes the concrete existence of man, while the moral law is treated as abstract and disembodied, incapable of responding to the demands and problems of individual cases.[29] Under this system, the circumstances that subjectively mitigate man's moral responsibility are destined to multiply. Simultaneously, the perfection of married life as obedience to God's commandment to live holily is dismissed as an unreachable ideal for life and is thus deferred to eternal life. The crack between this life and eternal life expands ever wider, which makes it difficult to look to the afterlife.

Sadly, a linguistic shift that characterises the entire Exhortation contributes to this crack. Cardinal Schönborn, in the press conference presentation of AL, and Fr. Spadaro, in his commentary on the Exhortation, both underlined this novelty of language. Schönborn said that AL is primarily "a linguistic event,"[30] while Spadaro stressed that "the style itself of AL is bound to the need of a 'renewal' and, yet more, of a true 'conversion' of language."[31] Soon after, Spadaro linked Pope Francis's style to that of the Synods and Vatican II:

> Already in the synodal context the desire had emerged to not be limited to normative or condemnatory language, but to use that positive and open language proper to the Council, gauging a specific pastoral approach in the light of the style of Pope Francis. [...] The language of mercy incarnates the truth in life.[32]

This linguistic shift creates many problems, ultimately leading to a kind of dogmatic nominalism. Words no longer have real meaning but represent certain conventional sounds; their true

---

29 Pius XII responds to this easy objection in an enlightening manner in the cited discourse (see note 20), noting that it is exactly by virtue of its universality that the moral law is capable of intentionally embracing all the particular moral cases. In some instances, it does this in such a precise and exhaustive manner that the conscience sees immediately and without difficulty the decision to take.
30 See note 10. [Translation ours.]
31 A. Spadaro, "*Amoris Laetitia.*" *Struttura e significato dell'Esortazione apostolica post-sinodale di Papa Francesco*, cit., 127. [Translation ours.]
32 Ibid., 128.

scope of content is reserved to a few individuals while the many are subjected to developing hermeneutic processes of understanding. This problem began many years earlier, precisely with the Second Vatican Council. Now is the time for theology to face the problem systematically, before the gift of Pentecost degenerates into Babel.

3

Nominalism:
THE GREAT TEMPTATION OF THESE DAYS

A SPIRITUAL BATTLE

Christian life is a spiritual battle, as St. Paul admonishes us. In Ephesians 6:10, he describes in the Christian's battle: "Finally, grow strong in the law with the strength of his power. Put God's armour on, so as to be able to resist the Devil's tactics, for it is not against human enemies that we have to struggle but against the sovereignties and the powers who originate the darkness in this world; the spiritual army of evil is in the heavens. That is why you must rely on God's armour or you will not be able to put up any resistance when the worst happens or have enough resources to hold your ground."

Here, St. Paul provides a sketch of the spiritual battle. Let us first consider why Christian life is a spiritual battle. We have begun this Lenten period by reading the Gospel in which Jesus was tempted by the Devil (Mt 4:1-11). This Gospel passage gives us a clear picture of Lent, because it is actually a description of the whole Christian life. We are reborn as Christians in the sacrament of Baptism through our rejection of the devil, and the whole Christian life becomes a fight against the devil and the secular world, a world which tries to drive us away from our Lord Jesus Christ. In addition to these two, there is also a third enemy: our flesh, that is, our earthly and material existence, pining for those things which do not endure forever. The Christian has several enemies to fight against—the flesh, the world, and the devil—in in what is considered spiritual combat.

Today, one sees more than ever that the enemies of Christianity always remain the same: the devil, the world, and the flesh. These enemies are both intellectual and physical, or corporeal. *Intellectual* means that these three enemies together try to stimulate our spiritual appetite to know something different from what mankind holds as true and good. These enemies help each other in fighting against Christians, against the way of life in line with the Gospel. The intellectual suggestion then becomes a corporeal temptation, a longing for goods to satisfy our material hunger, as Christ was tempted to turn stones into bread. The enemies normally use an attack on the soul to get to the body, but can sometimes attack from the opposite direction: from the body to the soul. In either case, body and soul together become the object of trials and temptations.

For example, a false ideology, such as Communism, entrenched in the intellect negatively affects man's material life: depriving man of his freedom causes a deeper poverty, affecting his whole standard of life. Man cannot live on bread alone. On the other hand, material poverty and hunger have frequently been reasons to look for an ideology which could definitively rescue man from this corporal indigence. As a result, material indigence and even corporal slavery still persist where freedom is denied and religion, condemned as the cause of all evil, is forbidden.

All three enemies work together to teach us something new — something amazing, and interesting. However, if we examine this newness carefully, we discover there is something in it which is wrong, but also old.

One temptation which has arisen in a new way, but which at heart is very old, is *nominalism*. Of course, *pelagianism* is also prevalent today. Pelagianism is the effort to do everything without grace, relying only on our own capability: we can make it; we do not need God; we do not need any grace from Christ. Yes, this is a terrible temptation that has reared its head once again. Pelagianism was the heresy spread during St. Augustine's time, in the fourth and fifth centuries. In my opinion there is something deeper behind it, which is more intellectual than theological — more philosophical — and this is nominalism.

NOMINALISM: KNOWLEDGE AS NONSENSE

What is nominalism? It is a philosophy which began to spread around the end of the Middle Ages and continued to gain traction through the time of the Reformation. Luther was

Nominalism

a disciple of nominalism; he built his new theology on this way of thinking.

Nominalism holds that truth is mere sound—*flatus vocis*, that is, the sound of the voice. Within this framework, there can be no correspondence between human intellect and reality. Therefore, knowledge does not express reality but is merely a conventional way of granting common identities to existing things. Truths are only words; doctrines of faith are only ways of expressing conceptually what the Church believes, but no one can be sure whether there is any real bond between these doctrinal expressions and truth. We are left only with a manner of speaking; we only have sounds without any substance.

For example, let us consider the word *mercy*, which is fundamentally expressing the infinite love of God. God is mercy, but in our time, in our homes, in our parishes, what does mercy mean? In the Italian Senate they recently approved the same-sex union law. One of the politicians, who is considered very Catholic and is supposed to be a leading thinker, said that this was the right time to approve the same-sex union law because otherwise it would have been approved by enemies of the Church, who could have made it worse. Further, he claims that we are living in a time of mercy. His statement contains two errors: the law regulating same-sex unions is good, and mercy has a new meaning, one that justifies sin. The reason his party put all their efforts into supporting this law, a law against nature, is mercy! What then does mercy mean?

Nominalism judges truths and things only according to their appearance. Because the words expressing them produce a sound, they exist, but essentially speaking those words are empty, meaningless. The only meaning they have is whatever we give to them. Now, the word *mercy* could even justify a lifelong union lived in sin, because, in the end, God is merciful. But what is the relationship between mercy and justice? Nominalism cannot answer. This example is one of many that helps us better understand what nominalism is. It ultimately deprives things of their essence and turns everything into mere appearance.

The enemies of our spiritual life today gather together in order to fight against the true expression of Catholic faith, which does not only say something about God but is the expression of God's intimate mystery revealed to us by Sacred Scripture and Tradition. Moreover, faith is not only a logical expression, but is first and foremost belief in reality. Reality precedes logic, and logic can express something only because that thing truly exists. Faith means belief in God, and all the doctrines believed by an act of faith are realities. Believing that God is mercy is not merely imputing meaning to empty words, which can easily fall into contradiction, but it is accepting the reality of God's mystery, his love that through sanctifying grace truly makes us a new creation. Mercy is God's forgiving love, but there is no forgiveness without reparative justice by being truly repentant of sin. In a nominalist environment mercy could forgive sin without any repentance or even, at man's convenience, simply cover the sin, hiding it under the mantle of God's goodness. Nominalism is a way of speaking without being.

This kind of nominalism is very attractive. You can say everything you want but it is just *babble*. Anyone can say whatever he likes because he is only speaking empty words, but every idea must remain in this unintelligible sphere. Everybody in our culture is invited to express what he likes, because in the end what he likes is nothing. The logical conclusion of this line of thinking is that in the end God himself is nothing. In fact, the highest expression of nominalism is: "God is a mere nothing." God is only a *flatus vocis*. You can say "God," you can say "Lord have mercy, Christ have mercy," but what does it mean? It is a nice way to spend your time, a soothing dream, but ultimately these words would have no content because their content does not exist.

Nominalism is the enemy of our faith, of our spiritual life. Related to nominalism is another intellectual disease, which Pope Benedict XVI stigmatised at the beginning of his pontificate: the *dictatorship of relativism*. These two diseases are close friends. Nominalism ends in relativism; vice-versa, relativism paves the way for considering things only as mere sounds.

Relativism is the enemy of truth. It is a philosophy which holds that nothing is really true or better; no truth has consistency to endure. Relativism is another compelling system of thought that has taken hold of our culture. Since nothing is

Nominalism

true, each person can express his own thought, choose how he wants to live his life, decide what is good and bad, all on his own. Truth is only babbling, mere sounds.

We must fight against this enemy. This is truly an intellectual and spiritual enemy of our Christian life. This kind of dictatorship—because it is a dictatorship in our culture—is stealing ground, day by day, from under our feet; there is no longer any foundation for the truth, because all truths are only sounds, only modes of speech. God, faith, supernatural life, grace, and mercy, are only words, suddenly deprived of their essence. Words attempting to address these concepts are reduced to empty expressions. Life itself is thus emptied. It is urgent to fight against this enemy of our Christian life.

Consider that if nominalism were true, all man's efforts to know reality would be mere foolishness. However, the deep desire of man is not only to say something, as when we sing a beautiful song, enjoying its melody and its rhythm, but to know the truth, to give an answer to the main questions about human existence. Everybody is looking for an answer to a fundamental question: *Why life? Why the universe?* None of these questions can be satisfied by nominalism. Nominalism abandons the truth, delaying the answer about the meaning of life to infinity. Nominalism denies the truth, but this denial is not human.

THE LUTHERAN ROAD THROUGH NOMINALISM

I mentioned that Luther was in favour of this philosophy. Why? For Luther reason is diabolical and corrupted by sin, and as a result, it cannot express the natural truth; everything that can be known is discovered only through faith, without any support from reason. However, faith without reason is easily corrupted into belief without attending to the content of belief. The human act of assenting to God is important, and not just the supernatural act of accepting God's revelation. 'Faith alone' quickly became faith without truth. The truths of faith and the mysteries of Christian life, mixed with this fideistic (only faith) attitude, were completely spoiled. Luther's claim that the more you believe the more easily you are saved was practically the manifesto of a theological nominalism, where what really matters is *my conviction* to believe, not my assent to God's truth. Faith is reduced to a mere feeling.

Moreover, what truly mattered to Luther was finding a sure path to justification — that is, believing in order to become just. How can I be justified in God's sight? I can only be justified by believing or feeling that God is justifying me. Again, how can I be justified, and be certain of it? By strongly believing that God in his salvific mercy is justifying me. This is a vicious circle; this way of thinking treats God as one who should grant something to me. But what is justice? What is mercy? They are truths that I need in order to be saved. For Luther the justice of God is his salvific mercy, but what are they in themselves? We do not know. Luther does not know.

Faith becomes a feeling in my life. What is faith in itself? And what is Christian life? In effect, in this great nominalist panorama, we do not know anymore; we only know that faith is something important for me when I need it. It is important for me, for my life, to bridge the yawning gap between my feelings and the nonsense surrounding me. If my reason is unable to know the truth, the mysteries of faith become nonsense. Thus, nominalism is certainly a major enemy of our Christian life. Let us undertake a spiritual combat to fight against it. How?

We said beforehand that truth is something necessary to live. Truth leads us to discover reality, to give definitive answers about our lives. Nominalism denies that truth satisfies our lives. But man cannot live without looking for the truth. Life would be completely empty, meaningless, without truth. God is truth. God is love. When we say that God is truth, we say that God is the Supreme Being. By affirming that *God is* we say that He is being itself. He is the reality. It is not something imagined, not an empty saying. *God is.* Without God, nothing has its own existence; this is the very basis for our Christian life. If we do not understand that Christian life is not only a title, that God is not only the sound of my prayer, but that God is, that Christian life is a whole life lived in Christ, we have missed the whole point. We are wasting our time even going to Church. Why do we go to Church? For this reason: to find eternal life.

Nominalism

We have to take up arms in this spiritual combat, understanding firstly who the enemy we are fighting against is. The enemy is not only terrorism, ISIS; the enemy is something deeper behind all of those evils. It is a spiritual enemy; it is both intellectual and corporeal. If God is only a name, only a word, then everything is permitted. The only thing left to think about then is filling our bellies!

We have to know that our battle is not against creatures of flesh and blood but against powers, the sources of darkness in this world. There is no greater darkness than the blackness that is produced by this way of empty thinking. We have to enter into this battle, especially during this grace-filled time of Lent. We have to fight against these enemies.

We will conclude this reflection by quoting St. Gregory of Nyssa, the brother of St. Basil the Great: *"Man gets the likeness of the things he is fixed on."* In our spiritual life, in our Christian life, we assume the likeness of the things we are fixed on. If we understand that life is warfare, we can fix our eyes only on the truth, on Christ. If we fixate our life on the truth, we will receive the likeness of that truth. We have Christ, we have the likeness of Christ, and so we have everything. We are made in God's likeness; we have to strive, in this spiritual battle, to become ever more Christ's likeness. If we now fix our eyes on Christ, who said, *"I am the way, the truth, and the life,"* we will receive that likeness. If we think, as many do nowadays, that Christ is only a word, that faith is only a means for our own ends, something just to give us relief in this valley of tears, then, in the end, we will receive the likeness of nothing.

Let us entrust everything we have and ourselves to Our Lady. May she help us discover the enemy and undertake this spiritual combat. Final victory depends on our efforts, aided by the grace of Christ. Whether there will be a restoration of Christianity in our completely secularised Western World depends upon the way and the effort by which we are prepared to fight for Christ, fixing our eyes on Him alone.

4

Martin Luther 500 Years Later: Prophet or Revolutionary?
KEY-POINTS OF A THOUGHT SURPRISINGLY CURRENT

THE YEAR 2017 MARKED THE QUINCENtenary of Martin Luther's protest against the Catholic Church with his 95 theses in Wittenberg. October 31, 1517—supposedly the day when Luther nailed his theses to the door of the Cathedral—is commonly marked as the beginning of the Protestant Reformation, although not all historians share this view. In fact, the real Lutheran turning point is not found in Luther's protest against indulgences, but rather in his "tower experience" (or of "the latrine," as Luther also puts it (see Table Talks, 3232c)). This experience sets up the *Durchbruch*, the *compelling passage* to the Reformation, and will become "official" in the year 1520, when Luther composed his *De Captivitate Babilonica Ecclesiae*, which presents his new doctrine about sacraments in relation to grace.

The anniversary has been greeted with unexpected emotion and enthusiasm in the Catholic world. For example, Cardinal Kasper, in a recent booklet on Luther from an ecumenical perspective,[1] has encouraged us to look at the former Augustinian monk as a new St. Francis of Assisi who simply wanted to live the Gospel with his brethren. According to Kasper, Luther should be enumerated "in the long tradition of Catholic reformers that have preceded him." More recently, Msgr. Galantino, the secretary of the Italian Bishops' Conference, said that "the

---

1   W. Kasper, *Martin Lutero. Una prospettiva ecumenica* (Brescia: Queriniana, 2017); or. Ger. *Martin Luther. Eine ökumenische Perspective*, Patmos, 2016). Cardinal Kasper numbers Luther among those of "the long tradition of Catholic reformers who preceded him." Ibid., 27.

[Lutheran] Reform was, is and will be in the future an event of the Spirit."[2]

Many writers and scholars praise Luther as a "Catholic dissident." This is the title of Peter Stanford's book, in which he christens Luther, among other titles, "the Prophet of Vatican II" since he was the first to root the equality of the people of God in a *shared priesthood* of all Catholics. "That's pure Luther,"[3] Stanford says, perhaps not remembering that the common priesthood of all the faithful is not a *shared one* horizontally speaking, as in Luther's understanding, rather a consecration of all people in Christ through their baptism. Further, the common priesthood is ontologically distinguished from the sacrament of holy orders and hierarchically subordinated to it in order to comply with its nature—exactly what Luther denied with his new theological vision of a Church without hierarchy (basically without the Pope) and without holy orders, which he considered a source of power for the Romanists. Luther wanted a Church without the papal magisterium in order to interpret the Sacred Scriptures without mediation. He claimed his own authority to interpret based on a personal understanding of the Bible. The only way to tear down that Roman wall, however, was to abolish the sacrament of holy orders and to claim everyone was a priest, a bishop, even a pope.[4] The shared priesthood of Luther

---

2   This surprising statement was made by Msgr. Galantino during a Conference held at the Lateran University in Rome on October 19, 2017, as reported by the Sir News Agency: https://agensir.it/quotidiano/2017/10/19/riforma-500-anni-convegno-alla-lateranense-mons-galantino-la-chiesa-da-riformare-e-una-chiesa-crocifissa/.

3   P. Stanford, *Martin Luther: Catholic Dissident* (London: Hodder & Stoughton, 2017), 20.

4   Luther's *Address to the Christian Nobility of the German Nation Concerning the Reform of the Christian Estate* (1520) is central to this complete reset of the theology concerning the hierarchical structure of the Church and the new position on the Magisterium of the Church. Luther intends to tear down precisely three walls by which the Romanists "have protected themselves [...] in such a way that no one has been able to reform them" (LW 44,126). In his own understanding these walls are: 1) temporal power has no jurisdiction over the spiritual and the latter is above the former; 2) only the pope may interpret the Scriptures; 3) no one may summon a council but the pope. In truth,

is the result of this personal vision, which led to a search for a 'magisterial free zone' by calling on the nobility of the German nation and the sacraments. The following quote from Luther's *Address to the Christian Nobility of the German Nation* may help us better understand the essence of his position on the common priesthood, no longer recognizing any difference between a priest or bishop and a lay person:

> To put it still more clearly: suppose a group of earnest Christian laymen were taken prisoner and set down in a desert without an episcopally ordained priest among them. And suppose they were to come to a common mind there and then in the desert and elect one of their number, whether he were married or not, and charge him to baptize, say mass, pronounce absolution, and preach the gospel. Such a man would be as truly a priest as though he had been ordained by all the bishops and popes in the world. That is why in cases of necessity anyone can baptize and give absolution. This would be impossible if we were not all priests.[5]

However, one might wonder why this link between Luther and Vatican II arose. An American scholar, R. R. Gaillardetz, furnishes us with an answer:

> The Second Vatican Council was an event of unparalleled significance in the history of modern Catholicism. One has to go back to the Protestant Reformation to

---

the first wall in Luther's understanding is more than a political view. In fact, it is rooted in a new understanding of the sacrament of holy orders, now common to everybody, so that the difference between temporal and spiritual as well as clergy and laity might disappear. Luther writes: "When a bishop consecrates it is nothing else than that in the place and stead of the whole community" (LW 44,127). Once the hierarchical constitution of the Church was abolished, it was easier to detach the Bible from her Magisterium and hand it over to everyone's subjective understanding.
5   LW 44,128.

find an event that matches Vatican II's impact on Roman Catholicism.[6]

Perhaps it is only about impact, but it is still not honest to assimilate Catholic teachings to Luther's revolutionary views. I wish to provide some clues to understanding this revolution—not a prophecy—agreeing with Richard Rex's point: that Luther established a new religion. In a recent piece in "The Tablet" he writes:

> The Papal legate and theologian Cardinal Cajetan intuitively identified the seeds of a new religion in it when he met Luther at Augsburg in October 1518. [...] As it turned out, Cardinal Cajetan got it right. It was a new religion.[7]

SOME HINTS ON LUTHER'S INTERIOR TORMENT

It is worth considering a detail from Luther's life before attempting to understand his vision. According to Heinz Shilling—a German historian whose biography of Luther is held as one of the most accurate—Luther prayed the rosary, meditated, and sang the Psalms to the point of exhaustion. Yet these strenuous exercises of piety led him to despair since, believing that he was not able to offer them as he should, he felt he was becoming the object of God's wrath without His forgiveness. Luther's despair was not about *mulieres*—it was not a problem of chastity—but a deep moral suffering, caused by the recognition of the infinite distance between himself and God.[8] The "tower experience" was not only an illumination of his mind but also liberation from a burden. His prayer in search of a merciful God was finally heard. In the tower, he instantaneously comprehended Romans 1:17, *"In it the righteousness of God is revealed,"* a moment he described later in one of his *Table Talks*:

---

6 R. R. Gaillardetz, *An Unfinished Council. Vatican II, Pope Francis, and the Renewal of Catholicism* (Collegeville: Liturgical Press, 2015) IX.
7 Richard Rex, *Martin Luther's new religion*, The Tablet (14 October 2017) 8. See also his book: *The Making of Martin Luther* (Princeton: Princeton University Press, 2017).
8 See H. Shilling, *Martin Luther: Rebell in einer Zeit des Umbruchs* (Munich: C. H. Beck oHG, 2012).

When I learned that the righteousness of God is his mercy, and that he makes us righteous through it, a remedy was offered to me in my affliction (n. 4007).[9]

This new understanding of the relationship between justice and mercy—that justice is only understood in light of mercy and as something passive that renounces punishment—is indeed the foundation stone of Luther's new Christian building. The fact that *mercy finally could be offered to him as justice through faith*[10] was both refreshing and convincing. This passage reveals two key points: 1) the disputable theological position subordinates justice to mercy so much so that justice loses its identity, and 2) Luther transformed his subjective search for a merciful God into the architectural principle of his theology. The second shift marks a revolution in theology and in the history of thought. In a sense it is the beginning of modernity—that is, the precedence of the subject over the object, the conscience over the good and even over God himself. The first seeds of the primacy of the subject and conscience over truth and goodness are planted. With this in mind, we turn to Luther's declaration at Worms before the Emperor Charles V of Augsburg (1521):

> Unless I am convinced by the testimony of the Scriptures or by clear reason (for I do not trust either in the pope or in councils alone, since it is well known that they have often erred and contradicted themselves), I am bound by the Scriptures I have quoted

---

9   LW 54,308.
10 In another *Table Talk*, Luther denies justifying faith is knowledge at all: "Faith justifies not as a work, or as a quality, or as knowledge, but as assent of the will and firm confidence in the mercy of God" (LW 54, 359-360). Luther in his work *Against Latomus* (1521), in which he tries to respond to strong criticisms from the University of Louvain, says the following about mercy that covers up ungodliness: "What then, are we sinners? No, rather we are justified, but by grace. Righteousness is not situated in those qualitative forms, but in the mercy of God. In fact, if you remove mercy from the godly, they are sinners and really have sin, but it is not imputed to them because they believe and live under the reign of mercy, and because sin is condemned and continually put to death in them" (LW 32,208).

and my conscience is captive to the Word of God.
I cannot and I will not retract anything, since it is
neither safe nor right to go against conscience.[11]

Cardinal Kasper would contest the designation of Luther as the Father of Modernity, for although both modernity and Luther place an emphasis on freedom, the freedom of modernity is 'autonomous' and Luther's freedom was limited to a search for God. Kasper points out the difference between the two freedoms:

> Luther's call at Worms about conscience was without
> doubt an important step forward in the modern his-
> tory of freedom, even if, in his case, it was not a call
> to an autonomous conscience, but to a conscience
> captive to God's Word.[12]

For this reason, Kasper does not see Luther as the forerunner of the Modern way, but as the last heir to the medieval thought about the religious unity of the *societas christiana*.[13] Yet, is there much difference between an *autonomous* freedom that has precedence over truth, and a *theonomous* one that is captive to the Word of God? The only distinction between the two consists in the different levels upon which they lay—the former on the natural level and the latter on the supernatural—but both are concerned with the precedence of the subject over the object, without the mediation of a metaphysical reason so dear to the medieval people. A freedom that is captive to the Word of God will be used to justify any other freedom, whether that be the freedom to contradict the perennial Magisterium of the Church or to cover one's sin or weakness in search of a Christ beyond the Church and the sacraments.

NOMINALISM OR GOD'S ARBITRIUM

Luther follows the philosophical stream of nominalism that flowed from the Ockhamism of Gabriel Biel (1410–1495),

---

11 LW 32,112.
12 Walter Kasper, *Martin Lutero. Una prospettiva ecumenica*, 43-44. [Translation is ours.]
13 See Ibid., 44.

although he later diverged from Biel's teaching on the doctrine of justification. Luther himself declares that his "dear master"[14] was William of Ockham (c. late 1200's–1350), a Franciscan philosopher and theologian who became professor at Oxford in 1319, although he did not agree with him on everything.[15] For Ockham, there are only individuals: "Anything one can imagine is, by itself, without anything being added to it, numerically one, singular thing" (*In Porphyr.* proem. sec. 2, ed. *Opera phil.* II: 10). Consequently, there are no natures or essences, and the only things that exist are singular entities created immediately by the will of God. Since the existence of each individual being is directly linked to God's will with no 'reason' in itself, divine will must be absolute. In other words, it simply manifests itself as it is, necessarily and with no understandable reason. The process of reasoning is ultimately useless because we can only know reality as a plurality of individuals without ever understanding the reason behind this plurality; the concepts with which we identify existing entities are simply conventional sounds invented for pragmatic reasons, only a *flatus vocis*. Therefore, the words we speak have no inherent meaning because there is no real link between them and reality; they can only point to something. Is this not a prevalent assumption today?

Luther makes this nominalistic view his own. He claims that only God is necessary and whatever he does is necessary and absolute, unable to be comprehended by human reason. Man cannot discuss what God has planned or does because there is no

---

14   LW 34,27.
15   The main issue that Luther holds against Ockham is to deny the necessity of grace in order to accomplish good works, or that the Holy Spirit would not be necessary for them. Cf. G. Ockham, *Sententiarum*, lib. ii, q. 19A; lib. iii, q. 8B; M. Luther, *Table talks*, n. 5134, LW 54,391. In fact, in order to exalt the free will, Ockham denied the necessity of sanctifying grace for good works. However, this did not turn him into a Pelagian, for, according to Ockham, these good works are useless to eternal salvation, which depends only on God's free decision (here again the bond with Luther). See E. Iserloh, *Gnade und Eucharistie in der philosophischen Theologie des Wilhelm von Ockham* (Wiesbaden, 1956), 77-133. Contrary to Ockham's position, Luther, in his *Disputation against Scholastic Theology*, says: "It is not true that God can accept man without his justifying grace" (LW 31,13).

reason other than his divine will. Let us not forget that reason in itself is of no value to Luther: it would force him to consider a God beyond the simple (blind) acceptance of his healing mercy. This is a crucial point for understanding Luther's solution to the problem of freedom.

THE PROBLEM OF FREE WILL OR OF A SELF-CONTRADICTING GOD

For Luther, "free will is a pure lie."[16] This polemical statement comes from the end of *De Servo Arbitrio* (1525), which was written in response to Erasmus of Rotterdam's attack on Luther, *De Libero Arbitrio*. Even still, near the end of *De Servo Arbitrio* (literally *The Servant Will*), Luther actually commends Erasmus for tackling the only real problem at stake, emphasizing that even the issue of indulgences is not as essential as this vital question about the absence of free will:

> ... I praise and commend you highly for this also, that unlike all the rest you alone have attacked the real issue, the essence of the matter in dispute, and have not wearied me with irrelevancies about the papacy, purgatory, indulgences, and such like trifles (for trifles they are rather than basic issues), with which almost everyone hitherto has gone hunting for me without success. You and you alone have seen the question on which everything hinges, and have aimed at the vital spot; for which I sincerely thank you, since I am only too glad to give as much attention to this subject as time and leisure permit. If those who have attacked me hitherto had done the same, and if those who now boast of new spirits and new revelations would still do it, we should have less of sedition and sects and more of peace and concord.[17]

Free will does not exist, but is only man's pride challenging God. In the text, Luther explains that if man possessed free

---

16 LW 33,18.
17 LW 33,294.

will, he would be able to grasp God's inscrutability. However, since God is unfathomable, it follows that man is not free and whatever he does he is *obliged* to do. The obligation in the end comes from God's necessity. In other words, there is no free will, but only necessity.

> For all men find these sentiments written on their hearts and acknowledge and approve them (though unwillingly) when they hear them discussed: first, that God is omnipotent, not only in power, but also in action (as I have said), otherwise he would be a ridiculous God; and secondly, that he knows and foreknows all things, and can neither err nor be deceived. These two points being granted by the hearts and minds of all, they are quickly compelled by inescapable logic to admit that just as we do not come into being by our own will, but by necessity, so we do not do anything by right of free choice, but as God has foreknown and as he leads us to act by his infallible and immutable counsel and power.[18]

We can only accept this necessity on the basis of faith, which enables us to embrace even contradictions and therefore moves us to trust completely in Christ's saving power. Luther, in the first part of *De Servo Arbitrio*, offers two basic reasons why God deprives us of the use of free will. The first is *humility* and the other *blind faith,* which is strengthened by God's contradictions:

> First, God has assuredly promised his grace to the humble [1 Peter 5:5], that is, to those who lament and despair of themselves. But no man can be thoroughly humbled until he knows that his salvation is utterly beyond his own powers, devices, endeavours, will, and works, and depends entirely on the choice, will, and work of another, namely, of God alone. For as long as he is persuaded that he himself can do even the least thing toward his salvation, he retains

---

18   LW 33,191.

some self-confidence and does not altogether despair of himself, and therefore he is not humbled before God, but presumes that there is — or at least hopes or desires that there may be — some place, time, and work for him, by which he may at length attain to salvation. But when a man has no doubt that everything depends on the will of God, then he completely despairs of himself and chooses nothing for himself, but waits for God to work; then he has come close to grace, and can be saved.

[...]

The second reason is that faith has to do with things not seen [Heb. 11:1]. Hence in order that there may be room for faith, it is necessary that everything which is believed should be hidden. It cannot, however, be more deeply hidden than under an object, perception, or experience which is contrary to it. Thus when God makes alive he does it by killing, when he justifies he does it by making men guilty, when he exalts to heaven he does it by bringing down to hell, as Scripture says: "The Lord kills and brings to life; he brings down to Sheol and raises up" (1 Sam. 2:6). This is not the place to speak at length on this subject, but those who have read my books have had it quite plainly set forth for them.

Thus God hides his eternal goodness and mercy under eternal wrath, his righteousness under iniquity. This is the highest degree of faith, to believe him merciful when he saves so few and damns so many, and to believe him righteous when by his own will he makes us necessarily damnable, so that he seems, according to Erasmus, to delight in the torments of the wretched and to be worthy of hatred rather than of love. If, then, I could by any means comprehend how this God can be merciful and just who displays so much wrath and iniquity, there would be no need of faith.[19]

---

19 LW 33,61-62.

Martin Luther 500 Years Later: Prophet or Revolutionary?

The contradiction itself justifies faith and reveals to man his creatureliness and his weakness in the face of God's majesty. According to Luther, God shows himself for what he really is precisely in contraposition (or contradiction), i.e., *sub contraria specie*. Luther inaugurates a dialectical process which is a polarization of the veiling and unveiling of the mystery. The power of God can only be understood in the total weakness and abandonment of the Cross, just as the grace of his love is only discovered in the very act of rejecting it through the sins and offences of mankind. The theology of the Cross is essentially the continual contradictory *revelation and concealment* of God.[20] Love requires hatred to be fully revealed to a soul, just as faith requires its negation and must even be held in captivity by man's doubts and sins. The more obscure faith is, the more convincing it is. Although it might sound burdensome, God can only be appreciated as God when his negation is affirmed. God's negation is sin.

Christ can only be loved as a loving Savior if he permanently fights against the devil.[21] Strictly speaking, one cannot have a clear idea of Christ without the devil. However, according to Luther, Christ has become a sinner himself. In his *Lectures on Galatians* (3:13) he writes:

> And this is our highest comfort, to clothe and wrap Christ this way in my sins, your sins, and the sins of the entire world, and in this way to behold Him bearing all our sins. When He is beheld this way, He easily removes all the fanatical opinions of our opponents about justification by works. For the papists dream about a kind of faith 'formed by love'. Through this they want to remove sins and be justified. This is

---

20 See Giovanni Iammarrone, *Le teologie della Croce di S. Paolo, Martin Lutero e Jürgen Moltmann. Loro contestualità e precomprensioni*, in «Doctor Seraphicus» 52 (2005) 26. See also LW 33,287, which contains Luther's *De Servo Arbitrio*, which reflects on the fact that throughout Scripture Christ is presented in the context of *contrast* and *antithesis*. All that is without the Spirit of Christ is under Satan, error, sin, death, and God's wrath.
21 See Ibid.

clearly to unwrap Christ and to unclothe Him from our sins, to make Him innocent, to burden and overwhelm ourselves with our own sins, and to behold them, not in Christ but in ourselves. This is to abolish Christ and make Him useless.[22]

Christ can save no man from hell unless Christ himself is condemned to hell by man's sins. Luther persists in his conviction that sin has entered Christ and, through the Lamb of God, sin has entered God himself. Sin therefore damns Christ, although, by virtue of his eternal righteousness, he is victorious in the end.

> Not only my sins and yours, but the sins of the entire world, past, present, and future, attack Him, try to damn Him, and do in fact damn Him. But because in the same Person, who is the highest, the greatest, and the only sinner, there is also eternal and invincible righteousness, therefore these two converge: the highest, the greatest, and the only sin; and the highest, the greatest, and the only righteousness. Here one of them must yield and be conquered, since they come together and collide with such a powerful impact. Thus the sin of the entire world attacks righteousness with the greatest possible impact and fury. What happens? Righteousness is eternal, immortal, and invincible. Sin, too, is a very powerful and cruel tyrant, dominating and ruling over the whole world, capturing and enslaving all men. In short, sin is a great and powerful god who devours the whole human race, all the learned, holy, powerful, wise, and unlearned men. He, I say, attacks Christ and wants to devour Him as he has devoured all the rest. But he does not see that He is a Person of invincible and eternal righteousness. In this duel, therefore, it is necessary for sin to be conquered and killed, and for righteousness to prevail and live. Thus in Christ all sin is conquered, killed,

---

22   LW 26,279.

and buried; and righteousness remains the victor and the ruler eternally.[23]

Thus, contradiction is finally justified in a self-contradicting God (*selbstgegensetzung Gottes*), who, in order to save me, has to place himself against himself: the battle of sin and grace! This claim paves the way for Hegel's understanding of the life of the *spirit* (*der Geist*) as a dialectical process where affirmation is overcome by negation in order to find its synthesis in a wider and better good (the dialectical sum of good and evil).

This theological formulation of contradiction elevated to a principle of knowledge overturns the so-called negative theology in favour of a theology of a self-contradicting God: grace and sin can co-exist because, ultimately, they are rooted in God's opposing the intellect to his will. Therefore, humans are not free to choose not to sin, and God is not bound by any rational disposition but is free to act only according to his divine (arbitrary) will, infallible and immutable. Hence, we cannot do anything else than what God has ordained from all eternity. This is the root of Calvin's theory of predestination.

GRACE THAT COVERS SIN: THE PROBLEM OF JUSTIFICATION

The absence of freedom is the exaltation of faith. But can faith be satisfied without grasping anything of God's own mystery, blindly accepting the mystery of an eternal divine disposition? Is faith even free to step forward and say, "I believe"? For Luther, faith is not a free human act but imposed by necessity. Nevertheless, the role of faith (without knowledge) is highly valued in Luther's religious system. What is this about? Firstly, it is important to understand that, for Luther, original sin is above all a "radical sin," identified as the rebellion of the flesh. Since man sinned against God, the inclination to sin—the concupiscence of the flesh—is so strong that man lives perpetually in sin. Whatever man does is sinful. "Every good work is sin," writes Luther against Latomus (one of the theologians at the University of

---

23   LW 26,281.

Louvain), and "sin, as long as we live, inheres essentially in good works, just as the ability to laugh inheres in man."[24] Because of original sin man is captive to sin as such. Nothing brings about healing other than firmly believing that he has been saved by Christ. Faith is a "cordial trust," the act of entrusting one's heart to God through Christ.[25]

Moreover, faith is only understood as a personal effort, the conviction to believe in God, rather than the means by which we consent to believe in divinely revealed truths necessary for salvation. Faith is cordially believing that my sins have been forgiven and as a result, justice is poured out upon me as forgiving love. As a condition of this forgiveness, God will pretend not to see the sin that still remains in me.[26] Justice won't be present in me as my inheritance — nothing can adhere to human nature other than my sin — but it will be granted to me insofar as I firmly believe. Justice as such properly belongs to Christ — it is *iustitia aliena*, a justice that belongs to another. It is given to me as a temporal loan, whose duration is proportional to the intensity of my faith. Faith creates the possibility of a *joyful bargain* — *admirabile commercium* — in which I give Christ my sins and He gives me His justice.[27] In a sense, it is faith that produces grace and no longer grace that produces faith. But what about the first infusion of faith in baptism by grace? Given that faith is the necessary alternative to freedom, Luther has to conclude that grace is as necessary as faith. This is equivalent to saying that grace is no longer a gift but a right! However, if it is a right it is no longer grace, for *grace* means gratuitousness.

Luther's vision of human nature is one of deep pessimism: a man is condemned by the absence of his free will to commit sins that permanently infect his soul. No medicine, no hospital, is able to heal a sinner of this affliction so that he can return home and live a happy life. The man of Luther is permanently condemned to live in a 'field hospital' where only first aid and

---

24 LW 32, 168-169.186-187.
25 See LW 26,231: here Luther is commenting on Galatians 3,6.
26 See Ibid.
27 LW 48,12.

short-term remedies are available; no full check-ups or intensive therapies are offered, simply because they can have no real effect on the sick. These cures simply have no meaning. Nominalism is uncovered at the root of Luther's whole vision.

Can this theology, with its strong philosophical background, be understood as a reform of Catholic doctrine or is it rather the seeds of a new belief? I agree with Richard Rex: it is a new religion.[28]

---

28 See Richard Rex, *Martin Luther's New Religion*, 9.

5

Vatican II:
A PASTORAL CHALLENGE & THE KEY-PROBLEM OF ITS HERMENEUTICS

I. PASTORALITY, A DIFFICULT CROSSROAD OF LANGUAGE AND METHOD

For me, Vatican II was like a fascinating puzzle to solve. When I started to study its documents and the various, often contradictory, opinions about its reception and its impact on the life of the Church, I was struck deeply. I had one fundamental question: why is there such an emphasis on the last council of the Church, to the point of casting a shadow over all the previous councils? It is not as if the other councils were no longer true, but they seemed to have no role in this new ecclesiological structure. Vatican II has many sympathizers, but each one puts his own personal spin on its meaning and its place in the life of the Church. For some, it was a new era; for others, such as Karl Rahner, it is the "beginning of the beginning." In this almost revolutionary atmosphere, it should not come as a surprise that the position of some of its strong opponents should become ever more determined.

Many open questions about the most recent council still challenge us. For example, what is Vatican II for the Church and what is the correct relationship between the Church and the council? What does the last council mean to the whole structure of faith? Pope Francis has recently offered an answer to some of these questions:

> With the Council, the Church entered a new phase of her history. The Council Fathers strongly perceived, as a true breath of the Holy Spirit, a need to talk about God to men and women of their time in a more accessible way. The walls which for too long

had made the Church a kind of fortress were torn down and the time had come to proclaim the Gospel in a new way. It was a new phase of the same evangelization that had existed from the beginning. It was a fresh undertaking for all Christians to bear witness to their faith with greater enthusiasm and conviction. The Church sensed a responsibility to be a living sign of the Father's love in the world.[1]

It is somewhat surprising to hear a Pope speaking in these terms, using the same language as some of the progressive theologians at Vatican II. Nevertheless, after more than fifty years since the conclusion of Vatican II, there is still ambiguity about what it means "to talk in a more accessible way." There is a broad spectrum of possible meanings. For instance, we have moved from the language of Vatican II documents, in which the narrative, pastoral form is given precedence over the assertive, definitive form, to the new and paradoxical language of *Amoris Laetitia*. As we've seen above, the document's deliberate ambiguity promotes a more merciful interpretation of the doctrine concerning marriage and divorce. Perhaps most surprising in this case, the *ipsissima verba Christi*, which are recorded in the Synoptic Gospels and unequivocally condemn divorce and remarriage, are never quoted or explained. One might ask if this is part of the new way of speaking.

Perhaps the search for a new language in the Church is related to the more impressive action of tearing down the fortress-like walls, which protected the Church for centuries. One of the major goals of Vatican II was, as Pope John XXIII said in his opening speech, the attempt to discover a new way of presenting the perennial doctrine, characterized by a more merciful approach and more engaging language. He believed that language had become a problem within the Church. Pope John's opening request to the council was to examine the perennial doctrine of the faith in depth and to expound upon it according to the needs of our time (his time, 1962, already radically different from today). This request reveals a distinction in his

---

[1] Papal Bull, *Misericordiae vultus*, n. 3, April 11, 2015.

view between the deposit of Faith and the proclamation of those beliefs; John XXIII was differentiating between the perennial doctrine and presentation of doctrine. This programmatic discourse explains what is at stake: the Pope was asking the council to find a new approach to the doctrine, a new pastoral manner of proclamation.

This request was like opening a can of worms. The Council began a deep discussion which was not only a quest for new, more appropriate language — a quest that continues today — but also an attempt to understand what John XXIII meant by his distinction, which to many ears sounded not only new but problematic. Can we truly separate, even if only logically, the doctrine of Faith from its exposition? In other words, does the doctrine of Faith require appropriate language, a theological-metaphysical language, to express its mysteries? Pope John himself was not explicitly divorcing doctrine from language, but, as a result of his address — a result still developing in the Church — the doctrine was slowly watered down from its majestic language to facilitate a more pastoral engagement with the world, especially to further ecumenism. A similar refrain is often repeated nowadays: doctrine, as it is laid down in the Catechism, remains untouched but a new pastoral approach is urgently sought after. While the search continues, doctrine is frozen for some length of time. Unfortunately, as time passes, this pastoral freezing often softens doctrine, resulting in a new doctrine of pastoralism, or, more accurately, in a doctrinal pastoralism. However, *praxis* cannot exist apart from doctrine. Doctrine and praxis must exist side-by-side; otherwise, the pastoral practices can all too easily become dissociated and disconnected with the doctrines of the Church.

Therefore, the problem is language, which cannot be separated from the way of belief or the handing on of what we have received. Language cannot be separated from the contents of dogma but is an essential part of it and must be understood as a theological issue.

From the problem of language, we turn to the very core of the correct interpretation of Vatican II: the problem of pastoralism. Since the Council, the majority of the Church is dominated by pastoral concerns; *pastoral* is the keyword in nearly every problem of our time. Even the last two synods about marriage and the family were attempting to solve what has been called a pastoral problem — the irregular situations of divorced and civilly remarried people — but which inevitably affects the doctrine of three sacraments: marriage, confession, and holy Eucharist.

The correct interpretation of pastoral is related to many issues, such as what it means to be Catholic. Most people would probably say that welcoming refugees into our countries is what it means to be Catholic. Many would base their answer in teachings from Vatican II. It is astonishing that the solution to nearly every problem is found in the last council, even though the battle between spirit and letter continues.

Vatican II should help us face new pastoral challenges and answer related questions. For example, what does an enlightened pastoralism entail for the implementation of the only true faith in society? What must we do to evangelize all peoples? What answer shall we give to this continuous and massive Islamization of Europe? How should we respond to the horrific bloodbath throughout the formerly Christian world? May Vatican II lead us down the best pastoral pathway in this critical moment for the Church. Let us be truly pastoral!

2. THE INTERPRETATION DOES NOT EXPLAIN THE INTERPRETATION. WHICH HERMENEUTICS?

Hermeneutics, i.e., the interpretation of a text, is never the solution to the problem but only the means of reaching a solution; it refers to a basic principle that precedes the interpretation and development of the text. This principle is the faith of the Church, namely the *organic development* of her doctrine.

The problem is twofold. First, there is an interpretative problem. The texts of Vatican II — as every text, for that matter — are, according to Pope Benedict XVI, subject to two possible methods of interpretation, that of *discontinuity and rupture*, or that of *renewal in the continuity*. The choice of hermeneutic depends on our understanding of the Church. What is the Church? Is it a permanent synodality that becomes aware of itself in history through the extraordinary convocation of a council? Or a mystery that precedes time, becomes incarnate in history, and will later surpass its earthly incarnation in eternity? From a theological point of view, the hermeneutics born in an existentialist and post-metaphysical context must be grounded in the mystery one wishes to study. Vatican II must be interpreted in relation to the Church. Otherwise, we run the risk of transforming the method into a solution, creating a continuous and absorbing interpretation.

It is not enough to clarify the hermeneutic approach and choose what is consonant with it. We must examine the conciliar texts by employing the hermeneutical method. We cannot simply choose the hermeneutic of *renewal in continuity* to resolve the problem of the texts of Vatican II (admitting that such a problem has been recognized at the epistemological level), but we must apply the hermeneutic to reveal or demonstrate the continuity. If the method was the solution and not the point of departure, the choice of a hermeneutic would solve the problem. However, in Benedict XVI's discourse to the Roman Curia (December 22, 2005), after contrasting the correct hermeneutical principle to the erroneous one of rupture, he immediately demonstrates how to apply it with the example of religious liberty. He reaffirms that principles do not change, but the historical forms that bear those principles are subject to change. Therefore, continuity is in the principles, and mutability or discontinuity is in the historical forms. The problem, in Benedict XVI's judgment, is precisely the coordination of continuity and discontinuity, which are both bound up in interpretation, even if on two different levels. The current situation has already drastically shifted from the situation of the 1960s and 1970s. A frightening relativist aggression has replaced an open-minded and tolerant thrust towards the exercise of religious liberty, a shift which should prompt theologians to seek new possibilities for correctly exercising religious liberty in the external forum, concentrating more on God's truth than the choice between the varied religious panorama. This topic, however, requires a separate discussion.

Let us return to the problem of method. If we want to understand Vatican II correctly, we must interpret the documents in light of the Church's faith, the key criterion from which we begin and to which every theological interpretation returns. Simply choosing to adopt a hermeneutic to fit one's interests does not solve the problem of interpretation, whether one adopts the hermeneutic of rupture or continuity. For example, let us examine a doctrinal element in the decree on ecumenism, *Unitatis Redintegratio* n.11, the so-called hierarchy of truths. What does it mean? As it is formulated in this document, the principle may appear new and unfamiliar, as is typical of Vatican II. This proposition, which in turn serves as a criterion for interpreting Revelation, must be interpreted correctly. Is it claiming that certain truths are hierarchically subordinated because they are revealed less clearly than others or that they are less binding because they are not as important? On the contrary, in the system of revealed truths (defined or undefined by the Church), each truth does not have the same relationship to Divine Revelation, which means that each truth must be placed in particular relation to the four main dogmas of the Church, namely, the mysteries of the Trinity, of Christ's Life, Death, and Resurrection, of the Holy Spirit, and of the Catholic Church. For example, the Immaculate Conception of Mary is connected to God's Revelation through the dogmas of original sin and Christ's redemption of mankind. We would never say that the Immaculate Conception is less important or less revealed than the doctrine of redemption. The hierarchy of truths must be understood via the analogy of truth and not as the subordination of some truths to others. Therefore, using the hermeneutical criterion of continuity and interpreting the council in light of the Church's tradition, *analogia fidei* is the only correct reading of the hierarchy of truths, rather than using, as some theologians do, the precedence of praxis over theory. We can see the effect of emphasizing praxis over doctrine in the precedence of ecumenical dialogue over the one and unique truth of the Church — and thereby claiming that the unity of Christ's disciples, invoked by the Lord Himself, is more urgent than the unity of the Church constituted by her Divine Founder. The only way to use the hermeneutical principle correctly is for the constant beliefs of the Church to guide it. In fact, the only correct principle of interpretation for Vatican II is the uninterrupted Tradition of the Church. Tradition also protects us from reducing the whole of Vatican II to a hermeneutical problem, through an adaptation more or less favourable to modernity, which forgets the true reason for calling the Council. Fifty years after the last ecumenical Council, it is time to make room for faith rather than merely interpretation.

3. THE COUNCIL THAT POSES THE PROBLEM OF THE COUNCIL?

The hermeneutical problem of the Second Vatican Council did not originate after the close of the Council, or in the receptive phase of the conciliar magisterium, but during the conciliar meetings themselves. Surprisingly, the theme of the council's pastoralism, sometimes called *aggiornamento* (a word never used in the papal discourses during the council, but that John XXIII used in reference to the Code of Canon Law in his speech for the convocation of the Roman Synod, and consequently in reference to the new council), allowed for the shift from the schemas that were already prepared for the conciliar discussion to the new schemas that arose during this discussion and the heated theological disputes among the experts. For example, many at the council believed that the schema, *De Fontibus Revelationis* (On the Fount of Revelation) was not sufficiently pastoral and did not correspond to the intentions John XXIII expressed in his opening speech, *Gaudet Mater Ecclesia*. Similar instances repeated like a *leitmotiv* in the discussions. The Council needed to establish what *pastoral* actually meant and whether John XXIII had intended to juxtapose pastoralism (already understood per se in a new way) against the *modus operandi* of the previous ecumenical councils. The orators in session often returned to this issue, especially regarding the more important schemas, such as the one on the Church, which required an interpretation of the *mens* of the Pope. This requires an interpretation of the *mens* of the council itself. In fact, the interpretation of pastoralism, as used the opening speech, will orient the majority of the council and, subsequently, the votes. The meaning of pastoralism in the mind of the Second Vatican Council is a question of paramount importance.

I do not follow in the footsteps of Christoph Theobald in the French circle, of Hanjo Sauer in the German, or of Giuseppe

Ruggieri in the Italian, who make pastoralism itself the hermeneutical principle of Vatican II, reading the entire conciliar magisterium by its light. Rather, pastoralism itself is the problem, and the solution actually lies in the classic distinction between what is dogmatic and what is pastoral. While pastoral will undergo further analyses and clarifications through future challenges, its raison d'être is rooted in the dogma of faith and the one undivided Church (to act, one must first exist). For this reason, it cannot be the hermeneutical motive for the conciliar impetus towards a "new Church" or a "softer doctrine" that adapts itself to various situations. Praxis itself is linked to time and concrete situations, whereas the Faith precedes time and is protected and announced by the Church, enlightening and redeeming it. One relevant theological question remains: can we rewrite dogma in a more "pastoral way" to accommodate the current modern times? It does not seem that this is the case, nor what the Council actually desired. In the end, we must place faith and charity, reason and love, in right relation with each other.

Many individuals have a growing interest in understanding the true sequence of events at the Council, both historically and theologically. Certainly, this is a praiseworthy endeavor. In recent years, scholars have produced studies on the hermeneutical themes of Vatican II and the prior distinction of the conciliar magisterium according to the documental hierarchy. A dogmatic constitution is not a decree or a declaration. The two dogmatic constitutions *Lumen Gentium* on the Church, *Dei Verbum* on Divine Revelation, along with the constitution *Sacrosanctum Concilium* on the liturgy and the pastoral constitution *Gaudium et Spes*, are often hailed as the pillars of the whole magisterium of Vatican II. Each constitution contains different doctrinal content. *Gaudium et Spes*, unlike *Lumen Gentium*, cannot rise to the level of doctrine *stricto sensu* or *in toto*, because it presupposes some doctrinal principles; in this document, the Church explains her relationship with the modern world, which is constantly in flux. It is difficult to reconcile the two words that distinguish the document: *constitution* and *pastoral*. The council is clearly adopting a new method of teaching, which thus must have a corresponding hermeneutic. Furthermore, each of the two dogmatic constitutions exercises various levels of magisterium. The general tenor of the teaching is solemn/extraordinary or supreme in respect to the subject who teaches (an ecumenical council) and authentic, ordinary, in respect to the subject taught, deducing this from its re-proposition or initial proposition and from the manner in which it is taught. In order to understand the Second Vatican Council we must make distinctions and we cannot "put all our eggs in one basket."

We must examine another factor for correctly approaching the documents, namely, that a later declaration or a decree often reprises or deepens the study of themes taught in the constitutions. For example, the subject of ecumenism — the relationship with the Church of Christ, the Catholic Church, and other Christian communities or churches — examined in *Unitatis Redintegratio* deepens our understanding of the same theme in *Lumen Gentium*. For this reason, a dogmatic constitution is not a closed and definitive text, because another document of a lower juridical nature or an idea developed elsewhere can be used to complete its teaching. Let us examine a case in which the lower document explains the dogmatic constitution. The theme of the permanent diaconate in *Lumen Gentium* is revisited with a new and unfortunately problematic emphasis in the decree on missions, *Ad Gentes* (which speaks of "men who carry out the functions of the deacon's office" (n. 16), although these "functions" do not exist outside the sacrament). What does teach us about hermeneutics? Above all, we must be cautious in distinguishing between doctrines, how they are taught, and the nature of the document that explains them, while always bearing in mind the ever-present goal of the council: pastoralism.

In my other work,[2] I draw attention to other themes deserving theological attention. In studying Vatican II and its conciliar phases, a singular fact emerges. During the sessions of conciliar debates and especially in the Doctrinal Commission, more recent and modern doctrines — for example, episcopal collegiality, permanent married deacons, or the sacramentality of the Church — were

---

2 *Vatican II: A Pastoral Council, Hermeneutics of Council Teaching* (Leominster: UK, 2016)

proposed with notable zeal by skilled theologians to the Council Fathers, and were later incorporated into the magisterium. Yet, other doctrines, more ancient in their dogmatic development, and often commonly held — we can think of limbo, creation and the snare of evolution, or the members of the Church (how does one belong perfectly or entirely to the Church?) concerning the connection between the invisible mystery or mystical Body of Christ and the visible and hierarchical society or the social and historical body — were set aside because they were not yet mature and should be left to further theological discussion. Thus, the Council excluded some questions because they were disputed, while incorporating others. We ought to readdress the *status quaestionis* of many doctrines abandoned at the vigil of Vatican II and re-examine their relevance to the present day. They could help us resolve the superficiality that often reigns over the speculation and systematic reflection of theological knowledge.

To pose questions is the *proprium* of every science, including theology, which is the science of the Faith. Theology must be capable of raising questions, certainly not through embracing the Cartesian method, which desires to demonstrate faith by questioning it, but to clarify, as far as possible, the reason for its assumptions and to favor the development of the *intellectus fidei* — to read the faith from within, by entering into it. We cannot ask just any question; we must ask the right questions. In my latest work, I attempt to pose those questions which, in my opinion, still demand an answer and are vital for the object of our study.

4. PASTORALISM ON ITS OWN CREATES A PROBLEM RATHER THAN GIVING A SOLUTION

The problem of the council revolves around the issue of pastoralism, which is not a problem in itself but needs to be defined according to the mind of the council. If one simply applies its classical definition or adopts the interpretation of some influential conciliar theologians, then the word assumes more than one meaning, often exceeding its ambit. In the name of pastoralism, discussions were cut short; it dictated the agenda of the council's extraordinary magisterium was often planned and the proposal of doctrine, even if they were theologically young and should have been left to further debate. Another surprising factor emerges. Many praise pastoralism as an ecumenical effort, but it is almost always a one-way ecumenism with Protestants. And what about the Orthodox of the East? Some fathers saw in this pastoral choice more a wound, rather than an incentive, to unity than a new encouragement. For example, why was there an extremely long disquisition on the *Traditio constitutiva* of the Church, which had lasted for years, with the aim of toning it down, when it was the central and vital theme of Orthodoxy (above all in the liturgical ambit)?

Furthermore, we must consider the key problem: we cannot transform the object of study, that is, the new significance of the conciliar pastorality, into the same hermeneutical method we use to resolve the issue. The problem cannot be the method of resolution. I will offer some examples to show how the council fathers and theologians debated in the name of pastorality, which John XXIII proposed as the new framework for the entire magisterial structure. For this purpose, I present the definition of the word "pastoral" given by a conciliar father and a theological expert of the council's Doctrinal Commission.

The General Master of the Dominicans and one of the conciliar fathers, Fr. Aniceto Fernandez, presents the following definition of "pastoral" during the conciliar session:

> 1. The word "pastoral" is an adjective. It cannot be understood nor explained if not with regard to the substantive. The substantive admits a double case, and one must not mistake one for the other; a) it either means the substantive that is the pasture or food; b) or otherwise the substantive that is the method of administering food and pasture. 2. Therefore, the pastoral *munus* of the Council refers principally to the substantive that is the food or the pasture. In fact, the Council defends the truth, it proposes the truth. The truth is clear, perspicuous, it is what one would expect of it. The pastoral *munus* of each one

of us refers principally to the substantive that is the method. The conciliar doctrine belongs to the pastors, wholesome food to administer to all, attentive to the conditions of places, times and people. A simple way to the simple, a learned manner to the learned. [...] We must not seek a pastoral nature that is obtained to the detriment of the truth. Wherefore, if out of two formulas, one more pastoral but less clear and exact, and another less pastoral but clearer and more exact, without a doubt, the second is to be preferred in council. In pastoral praxis the first is chosen....[3]

In opposition to Fr. Fernandez's understanding of pastorality, which is in line with the traditional vision of theology and magisterium, E. Schillebeeckx, offers a more theologically personal interpretation:

> The *pastoral council* becomes *doctrinal*, precisely on account of its pastoral character. "Pastoral" calls for *doctrinal deepening*."[4]

Here the Council's pastorality clearly, rather than being food with which to nourish the faithful with the truth, becomes a "strategy" which makes the same doctrine blossom. Of course, not all the theologians shared in this vision, but the more influential and renowned did.

These two examples demonstrate why it is difficult to identify the meaning of pastorality in Vatican II. For this reason, I describe as *epiphania* (manifestation, apparition) those moments where mixture of doctrine and pastoral is made manifest — doctrine develops for a pastoral motive, not for doctrine as such, and is presented in a way that bears in mind certain external factors, especially the ecumenical afflatus. According to the distinction of Fr. Fernandez, the council already carries out the work of the pastor, that "translation" of doctrine that bishops and priests ought to implement with all-pastoral prudence and

---

3 In *Acta Synodalia* (=AS) I/3, p.237.
4 *The Council Notes of Edward Schillebeeckx 1962–1963*, Peters, Leuven 2011, p. 37.

solicitude. The language of *pastoral epiphanies* shows precisely how the Council's "principally pastoral aim"—as one deduces from the official comments of the Secretary of the Council or from the Council's Doctrinal Commission[5]—dictates the magisterial development of Vatican II and also limits presentation of the doctrine. Vatican II often consolidates itself on the ordinary authentic magisterium. It was certainly free to do so, but councils were customarily convoked not to begin teaching doctrines but to settle errors, define truths of the Faith, or teach them in a definitive and hence unreformable way. Here is the difference between Vatican I and Vatican II, which reveals itself precisely in this new fusion of pastorality and doctrinality. I intend to protect Vatican II from an excessive enthusiasm, which could generate a re-interpretation in light of the *pastoral epiphanies*, ultimately concluding that we are actually, for the first time, handling a pastoral council! In examining these epiphanies and attempting to apply a realistic hermeneutic, I maintain the traditional distinction between pastoral and dogmatic, recognizing one as the cause of the other and subordinating praxis to faith and dogma.

I examine the council's epiphanic pastorality in three areas: 1) in the intentions and formation of the doctrine regarding the relationship Scripture-Tradition in *Dei Verbum*; 2) in the aim and arrangement of the doctrine on the Church in *Lumen Gentium*; 3) in the intentions of the fathers and the formation of the Mariological doctrine in the chapter VIII of *Lumen Gentium*. The construction of the Marian chapter is one example of a council *in fieri*, fundamentally divided on the interpretation of the pastoral and ecumenical significance of its teaching. The conciliar Mariology, though rich and abundant, is emblematic of a problem in the council. With a disparity of 40 votes, the Council Fathers incorporated the Marian scheme, along with all its consequences, into the document on the Church. While the doctrine taught in the final constitution is magisterial, its correct hermeneutic must consider its formation and the *mens* that animated the fathers. Although Vatican II is undoubtedly a new council in various aspects, it cannot transform the Church itself into a new council.

---

5 Cf. AS II/6, 205; AS III/8, p.10.

5. NEITHER DOGMATIZATION NOR LIQUIDATION BUT DISTINCTION

It is particularly disconcerting to see how the Second Vatican Council has been "bent," not without deliberate coercions, to varied interpretations, all fundamentally due to an over-estimation of the last Council to the exclusion of the other previous councils, the Church's history, even the very mystery of the Church. If we accept the idea of a conciliar gap between the first and the third Christian millennium — as the so-called "Bologna School" does — then Vatican II certainly serves to fill this void. Undoubtedly, not every council was dogmatic like Trent and Vatican I, but Vatican II was the first council hailed as pastorally dogmatic or dogmatically pastoral. Some call it a new beginning or the North Star of the solemn and supreme magisterium of the Church, and then, to protect its new doctrines, they "infallibilize" them against the Council's intention. Why such tenacity on Vatican II? Perhaps it was supposed to be the banner for a new Catholicism, a transformed post-conciliar Church. Those who hold this view do not realise that it is to the council's detriment, reducing it to a dam, a "superdogma" that relativizes faith and morals.

By tracing the historical development of the idea of a council (see the first chapter of my book), it is clear that the juridical concept of "representation" — a council represents the Church — does not define a council in the strict sense (the conciliarists of the fourteenth century developed this concept to subordinate the Pope to the council). Instead, a council responds to the need, already felt at the first ecumenical Council of Nicaea, to defend the faith and teach the truth, the greatest spiritual gift. The issue of a council has never been its infallibility but the necessity to declare the truth.

Those who claim Vatican II is a break from Tradition, in my humble opinion, over-estimate the council, dogmatizing its doctrines, even those pastoral teachings about current issues. If, as some theologians judge, a solid biblical foundation is missing in order to establish religious liberty in the external forum as a foundation of a Christian State, which institutes "tolerance" for other religious practices, how much more unstable will the biblical foundation be if one holds all religions as equals in civil society, thereby leaving the responsibility of announcing the Gospel to the laity? Does the State no longer have any obligation towards God and the *religio vera*? I refer, to the example of positive religious liberty (exercised in the external forum) because it is one of the most debated subjects, whereas negative religious liberty remains biblically and traditionally explicit (no matter of faith can be forced on anyone's conscience). This discussion, among others, requires greater elasticity. Vatican II must be read and interpreted for what it is, according to its *mens*, and not according to a personal (political) inclination toward an ecclesiastical right or left, conservative or progressive. Already, in 1968, Dietrich von Hildebrand proved that a mere contraposition between conservatism and progressivism is sterile. You must choose either truth or prevarication, truth or a "spiritual house of cards."

For this reason, I have attempted to interrogate the council on its own terms. I have sought to rediscover—as far as possible—the *mens* of Vatican II on certain key doctrines. The theologian desires, above all, to understand the hierarchy of the magisterial teachings of the doctrines. Precisely because this order is not clear, we must systematically study the council's sources. Indicating each doctrine with the appropriate grade of magisterial teaching, each corresponding to both a theological note and a theological censure—I re-engage the topic of notes and censures that are so indispensable to theological discussion—, allows us to examine the conciliar doctrines in the proper mode. A correct understanding, doctrines are not yet definitively taught, paves the way for suggestions for an organic dogmatic progress, realized in any case by the Church's magisterium. These doctrines, which are among the most significant in the whole magisterial structure—Scripture-Tradition, membership in the Church, episcopal collegiality, the mystery of the Blessed Virgin Mary in Christ and the Church—can truly be denoted *"sententiae ad fidem pertinentes."* In other words, they are doctrines "upon which magisterium has not yet pronounced itself definitively, whose negation could lead to placing other truths of the faith in danger and whose truth is guaranteed by their intimate connection with revelation."[6] Subsequent dogmatic development is necessary for these doctrines to reach the grade *"definitive tenenda"* or, higher still, to be proclaimed as dogma of faith. Many theologians in council, only consider the sacramentality of the episcopate to be a definitive doctrine, but, even on this point, there is no unanimity.

Some might see the verification of the so-called *mens Sanctae Synodi* as a dangerous exercise, since Magisterium justifies itself. Divorcing the *mens* from the doctrine, however, would abolish the very existence of theology and contradict the General Secretariat's repeated invitations to read the proposed doctrines from the conciliar magisterium (not dogmatically defined or definitively held) with the spirit of the council itself, a spirit revealed in the subject of study and the manner of expression, in accordance with the norms of theological interpretation.

The distinctiveness of my work consists in my use of numerous first-hand sources in my attempts to faithfully interpret the doctrines of the Council. The expert reports of theologians of the Doctrinal Commission were of great importance to my work. In the hierarchy of sources, these should be placed above the personal diaries, directly after the Synodal Acts. They constitute the most authentic testimonies of what the theological mind of the council prepared for the discussions, modifying or improving them based on the council discussions, accepting or rejecting the so-called *modi* presented by the fathers. It is not difficult to find the theological theses promoted by the majority positions within the Commission. the step-by-step discussion of the Doctrinal Commission provides great epistemic help in correctly evaluating the Fathers' arguments in session. The fathers frequently depended on other theologians, but their theology did not always rely on the Church's Tradition. This is another factor to bear in mind, one that can settle many open discussions regarding the correct hermeneutics of the Second Vatican Council.

---

6 S. M. Lanzetta, *Vatican II, a Pastoral Council. Hermeneutics of Council Teaching* (Leominster: UK, 2016), 423–432.

6

The Renewal of the Permanent Diaconate in the Second Vatican Council
REQUESTS, RESULTS AND PROBLEMS

INTRODUCTION

In the aftermath of the First World War, a project was proposed to reintroduce the permanent diaconate as an ad hoc deputy ministry to aid the immense pastoral effort towards the needy, the imprisoned, the underprivileged, the homeless, etc. In an address to the Second World Congress of the Lay Apostolate (October 1957), Pius XII recognized the possibility of a permanent diaconate as an ecclesiastical ministry distinct from the priesthood (of bishops and priests), which would, however, require the laity to abandon their lay state and enter the clerical state. Pius XII judged that the time was not yet ripe for welcoming such an innovation, but the advent of the Second Vatican Council was a catalyst for all these latent hopes.

"The central argument for the revival," N. Trippen notes, "was the pastoral need in the face of the lack of priests, the central motive for those who were contrary was the fear about priestly celibacy."[1] On the other hand, H. Kramer, barely two years after the council, insists that "the shortage of priests cannot be the decisive reason for a renewal of the diaconate. It is for us an external symptom rather than an internal motive of our pastoral situation."[2] In any case, "the Council's point of view is that the

---

1 N. Trippen, *Die Erneuerung des Ständigen Diakonats im Gefolge des II. Vatikanischen Konzils*, in *Der Diakon*, eds. J. G. Ploger and H. J. Weber (Freiburg i. Br. 1980), 91.
2 H. Kramer, *Un nuovo tipo di diacono*, in *Concilio vivo. Bilancio del Concilio. La nuova immagine della Chiesa*, ed. B. Lambert (Milano

'pastoral need' (see Constitution on the Church, 29) must be decisive for the installation of the deacon."³

Vatican II was animated above all by motives of a more pragmatic nature in the re-establishing an ancient diaconal function. These motives then provoked gradual doctrinal development and the renewal of the diaconate in the Church. Thus arose one of the more significant problems in the post-conciliar period. The rehabilitation of the diaconal ministry required a theological development of the nature and mission of the deacon in the Church, a role scarcely understood when the Church solemnly postulated its resumption.

Thus we arrive at the heart of our examination: the limit which the Second Vatican Council imposes on itself but which in the end overcomes the council i.e., the insufficient dogmatic maturation of the doctrine of the diaconate. The International Theological Commission comments that "if Vatican II spoke cautiously and *ex obliquo* of the sacramental nature of the diaconate, it was not only from a concern not to condemn anyone, but rather because of the *incertitudo doctrinae*."⁴ While they desired to avoid removing every possibility of the opposing thesis in defining the sacramentality of the diaconate, the sacramentality itself was not sufficiently clear, and the demand for the re-establishment of the diaconate to overcome the scarcity of the clergy was pressing.

The Second Vatican Council was operating in this framework. Preoccupied with the restoration of the *principle of the permanent exercise of the diaconate* and not one of the specific forms

---

1967), 236 (or *Aspects nouveaux du gouvernement de l'Église. Un nouveau type de diacre*, in *La nouvelle image de l'Église. Bilan du Concile Vatican II*, ed. B. Lambert (Tours 1967), 158-172, 236).

3   Ibid., 238.

4   International Theological Commission (ITC), *From the Diakonia of Christ to the Diakonia of the Apostles* (2002), in: www.vatican.va/roman_curia/congregations/cfaith/cti_documents/rc_con_cfaith_pro_05072004_diaconate_en.html. In the note (n. 161) the precise text: "The biggest reason for this uncertainty lay in the fact of affirming 'diaconum non ad sacerdotium sed ad ministerium ordinari, atque nihil in hoc ministerio agere diaconum quin et laicus idem facere non possit'." We shall return to this below.

The Renewal of the Permanent Diaconate

which existed in the past,[5] the Fathers hoped that the theological and doctrinal understanding would grow.

1. THE WORK OF THE PREPARATORY COMMISSIONS

After consulting the bishops of the Catholic world, the religious superiors, and the superiors of the Catholic universities about the themes and suggestions they intended to propose to the imminent conciliar assizes (ante-preparatory phase), John XXIII established ten Commissions, coordinated by a Central Preparatory Commission, on June 4, 1960 to draft some constitutions to at the council.

341 of the 2150 *desiderata* evoked the theme of the permanent diaconate (PD), of which 222 encouraged the ordination of men already married and twelve openly rejected this proposition.[6] The principal concern for the majority of those in favor of re-establishing the PD was the shortage of priests. While the Europeans emphasized the charitable and social role of the deacon, the bishops of the third world focused on the deacon as minister of the Word, i.e., catechizer and preacher. However, many bishops (Spain, Poland, Great Britain, Belgium) expressed concern that a non-celibate diaconate would lead to the abolition of priestly celibacy. Diverse Italian prelates, though, noted that the laity already accomplished numerous diaconal tasks.[7]

Three of the ten preparatory commissions concerned examined the question of the diaconate.[8] The Commission on the Discipline of the Sacraments formulated a draft schema whose opening chapter, *On the Establishment of the Permanent or Stable Diaconate*, re-evaluated the minor orders and the diaconate, especially in areas where there was a shortage of clergy. Deacons

---

5   See Ibid., 303.
6   See *Acta et Documenta*, series I, Antepraeparatoria, vol. II, pars II, 115–132.
7   For a commentary on the facts, see P. Beltrando, *Diaconi per la Chiesa. Itinerario ecclesiologico del ripristino del ministero diaconale*, (Milano 1977). See also P. Weber, *Vatican II et le diaconat permanent*, in *Diaconat, XXIe siècle*, Actes du Colloque de Louvain-la-Neuve (13–15 September 1994), directed by A. Haquin and P. Weber (Bruxelles 1997), 80–82.
8   See *Acta et Documenta*, series II, Praeparatoria, vol. II/II, 140-473; vol. II/III , 211–601.

could potentially be married (with a minimum age of forty) but would be ineligible for a new marriage; they would minister to the bishop and the Church, assuming certain sacred functions such service at the altar, the administration of some sacraments, and the ministry of the Word. Pope John XXIII himself suggested the question of the PD, as Cardinal Gaetano Aloisi Masella (President of the Commission) attested in the presentation of the schema for its discussion.[9]

On January 17, 1962, the Central Commission examined this text. The first speakers were the Cardinals, who appeared divided. Ruffini, Siri, and Frings were hostile to the restoration of the PD, while Richaud, Döpfner, and Alfrink were favorable. Cardinal Jullien of the Curia, who opposed the proposal, argued that, although it was desirable to honor the catechists and laity who were active in the ecclesial movements, the schema ultimately redounded to a 'double clergy.'

This theme was also the subject of the Commission *De Missionibus*, which redacted a schema on the discipline of the clergy. It seemed most suitable to propose the re-establishment of the PD in a missionary context, above all to help the priests overloaded with pastoral work and thus incapable of providing for the evangelization of non-Christians. Cardinal Gracias, Archbishop of Bombay, strongly objected to this position. He argued that if the council desired to test the PD, it should do so in the European regions, not in the missions; the idea was alien to the religious sense of those who needed evangelization, but it had arisen in Europe. Cardinal Seper of Zagreb replied that a proposal made by numerous bishops could not be ignored. In his view, the non-celibate PD would serve the role of a *purgatio* for recognising the true candidates to the priesthood.

Finally, the Commission for the Oriental Churches commented on the PD, encouraging its re-establishment where it had become obsolete.

---

9 See the emphasis of G. Colombo, *Quale diacono in quale Chiesa*, in "Scuola Cattolica" 120 (1992), 302: "Rivisitando il cammino non agevole percorso dalla causa, è da pensare che il suo esito positivo, ma prima ancora la sua introduzione in aula conciliare, si debba sopra tutto alla raccomandazione forte dell'autorità papale."

The Renewal of the Permanent Diaconate

In this first phase of the debate, which prepared for the conciliar discussion, the definition of the problem of the PD and the possibility of its re-establishment emerges; here, the PD was affirmed as a matter of principle and not considered as an issue of fact. The *possibility* of re-establishing the PD in the Latin Church was discussed but remained bound to certain conditions. The Fathers of the Council later continued to consider the circumstanced for re-establishment in the council hall and the definitive documents. We can summarize the requirements for a restoration of the PD as follows:

> a) where necessity requires it to compensate for the scarcity of the clergy;
> b) where generally a *de facto* diaconate is already practised, in order to grant a specific sacramental grace;
> c) initial period of experimentation in order to be able to verify the proposal in principle.[10]

2. THE CONCILIAR DEBATE

The topic of the PD entered the conciliar discussion with a new schema on the Church, new since the Preparatory Commission's schema was rejected in the hall, even though the original contained, no reference to our topic. After notable contributions from theologians and alternative schemas, the Theological Commission arrived at the formulation of *De Ecclesia*, which was brought to the hall for discussion on April 22, 1963.[11] Chapter II of this schema addresses *ex professo* the question of the PD:

> At an inferior degree in the hierarchical ministry, the deacons assist the bishop and the priests; they serve the celebration of the sacrifice, they are extraordinary ministers of baptism and of holy communion and, in the measure in which this might be conferred on them by the competent authority, they can exercise various offices pertaining to public charity, preaching and administration. [...] The diaconate can, in the

---

10 See Ibid, 302–303.
11 See AS II/1, 215–281. [Translation ours.]

future, be exercised as a proper and permanent degree of the hierarchy, where the Church would judge it useful for pastoral needs, be it in certain regions or everywhere. In these cases it is incumbent on the pastors of the Church to determine whether or not these deacons ought to observe the law of celibacy.

The discussion of chapter II of the schema on the Church (schema II) lasted from September 30 until October 30,1963, when the Council opened her second session. The topic sparked a heated debate.

Cardinal J. Döpfner of Munich, who offered the first contribution,[12] gave the most autoritative and theologically sound arguments (united to some political reasons) in favor of the re-establishment of the PD. He maintained that the schema on the Church, which addressed the Church's hierarchical constitution, could not in any case remain silent on the order of the diaconate. Referencing the Council of Trent,[13] Döpfner understood the hierarchical tripartition of the sacrament of orders — episcopate, presbyterate and diaconate — to be divinely instituted and essential to the Church's constitution. He argued the sacramentality of the diaconate[14] based on the Council of Trent and, drawing in the German theological environment, proposed to ordain only those who already exercised *de facto* certain diaconal functions.[15] According to the German cardinal, the schema

---

12 See AS II/2, 227–230.
13 Decree on the Sacrament of Orders, can. 6: "*Si quis dixerit, in Ecclesia catholica non esse hierarchiam, divina ordinatione institutam, quae constat ex episcopis, presbyteris et ministris: anathema sit*" (DH 1776).
14 In this regard, the document of the ITC is more precise (2002): "The references by Trent to the diaconate (which it also refers to explicitly) need to be set within the general theology of the sacrament of Holy Orders. However, it is not entirely certain that the dogmatic declarations of Trent on the sacramentality and the sacramental character of the priesthood, to which Trent refers explicitly, include an intention on the part of the Council to define the sacramentality of the diaconate as well."
15 The exercise of a 'de facto diaconate' is ascribable to Karl Rahner. See M. Hauke, *Das spezifische Profil des Diakonates*, in *Forum Katholische Teologie* 17 (2001), 91. In fact Döpfner adds in his statement,

on the Church did not exceed what was already contained in Catholic doctrine. In fact, it is a less powerful proposal than what Trent declared, for Vatican II limits itself to affirming the possibility of re-establishing a PD and not its effective institution. Thus, the PD was dependent on a dogmatic argument, along with certain practical and disciplinary factors, including celibacy. While the law of celibacy is holy and to be preserved, Döpfner argued that it should not be an obstacle to a development that is dogmatically sound and pastorally necessary.

Similarly, Cardinal Suenens[16] argued that the diaconate appertains to the very constitution of the Church. Thus, it is necessary to begin any argument from the living faith in the sacramentality of the diaconate. Without resolving the exegetical controversy around the correct sense of Acts 6:3-6, Suenens maintains that since the apostolic and sub-apostolic age, the holy ministry was exercised in a degree distinct from the priestly and apostolic. This ministry had two primary duties: principally, assisting the bishops in the care of the poor and the sound coordination of the community; secondly, preparing the local Churches. In Suenens' opinion, if the PD were liquidated and diaconal offices were filled by the laity, we could forget that the Church, a supernatural society and the mystical body of Christ, is built on its ministries and on the grace preordained by God. Suenens' contribution focused not on the pastoral matter of the scarcity of clergy but on the sacramental matter of the ecclesial structure.

Cardinal Landázuri Ricketts of Lima,[17] speaking on behalf of the Peruvian Episcopal Conference offered a further development. Like Suenens, he disagreed with the proposition that the laity could assume the diaconal responsibilities for two reasons: 1) the sacrament of confirmation prepares a Christian for serving the Church in general, not for fulfilling particular offices; 2) the ecclesiastical hierarchy must develop integrally, not only in its higher degrees, and thus the grace cannot remain void in the diaconal order.

---

as a bibliographic suggestion, the text of K. Rahner, *Diaconia in Christo* (QD 15/16), ed. H. Vorgrimler, Freiburg i. Br. 1962.
16 AS II/2, 317–320.
17 AS II/2, 314–317.

A Spanish Father, Bishop Jubany Arnau,[18] contributed to the understanding of the diaconate as a sacrament. He inferred this from a few sources: 1) the dogmatic tradition, which shows the Apostles *ex dispositione divina* instituting the diaconate as an hierarchical degree; b) the liturgical documents which demonstrate that the diaconate is conferred with the imposition of hands; c) the Council of Trent (sess. XXIII, cann. 2.3.4.6). Therefore, he asked the council to affirm the diaconate in all its theological fullness.

In the debate hall, Cardinal J. K. Maurer (Bolivia) adds an essential detail: "the diaconate according to the common doctrine impresses on the soul an indelible and permanent character."[19]

Other Fathers, no less authoritative but with less convincing arguments, opposed the re-establishment of the PD. Some criticized the scarcity of arguments submitted in the request for a PD. According to O. McCann (Cape Town),[20] the theological presuppositions for the diaconate as a permanent and autonomous degree were not sufficiently illustrated. Cordeiro (Karachi-Pakistan)[21] questioned Suenens' thesis: if the diaconate is inherent it the Church's hierarchical structure and not desired merely for the exigencies of local Churches, how could its effective restoration to be left to the judgment of the Episcopal Conferences?

Doubting the need to re-establish a PD, Bishop Franić[22] questioned whether Christ immediately instituted the order of the diaconate. Far more probably, Christ instituted it *mediately* in the order of the presbyterate because he who has instituted the whole has also instituted the part. For this reason, the Church was free to confer the diaconate as part of the character of the presbyterate or to suppress it when it was not useful. Otherwise, there is no explanation for how the Church did, in fact, suppress a stable order. In Franić's view, the Church could confer the episcopate without the presbyterate and the presbyterate without the diaconate.

---

18 AS II/2, 580–586.
19 AS II/2, 410–414.
20 AS II/2, 810–812.
21 AS II/2, 711–712.
22 AS II/2, 378–384.

For both those in favor and those against the proposition, the scant doctrinal maturation of the theology of the diaconate was evident. The discussion became protracted and ever more intricate regarding the question of the diaconate and the entire second chapter of the schema on the Church.

At this point, Cardinal Suenens, one of the moderators of the Council, proposed a query asking the fathers if they wanted the schema on the Church to consider "the opportunity to establish a diaconate as a distinct and permanent degree of the sacred ministry, according to the usefulness of the Church in different regions."[23] 1,558 out of 2,120 voted in favor on October 29, 1963. A sub-commission was constituted to redact a new text. The sub-commission proposed to insert the topic of priests and deacons in the third chapter—maintained in the promulgated constitution—which spoke of the hierarchical form of the Church. Furthermore, they proposed to render the PD accessible to celibate young men and to leave the decision of non-celibate deacons to the Pope. The new text was prepared between March 6–11, 1964, and the definitive version was sent to the fathers for discussion and approval on July 3, 1964.

The new text was presented in the hall with the *relatio* of Bishop Henríquez Jiménez.[24] It emphasized the practical need that would be met by the re-establishment of the PD. Additionally, certain theoretical motives were expressed, and thus the *mens* of Vatican II was expressed in this regard: a) since the Council of Trent, the diaconate is understood to belong to the sacred hierarchy; b) the distinction between deacons and priests is that the first are ordained '*non ad sacerdotium sed ad ministerium*'; c) the prudence of the text regarding the sacramental character of the diaconate is evident: though such a sacramental nature is founded in tradition and the magisterium, the document only speaks of the "sacramental grace" of the diaconate to avoid condemning the thesis of a few recent authors, who disclosed some doubts on this point;[25] d) the privileged rapport of the deacon in

---

23   AS II/3, 537–575.
24   AS II/3, 214–218.
25   This aspect is clarified by the *Relatio* of the Doctrinal Commission, see note 36.

helping the bishop; e) finally, the inappropriateness of presenting this ministry as a palliative for the lack of priests.

On September 21, 1964, they began voting on various passages of the text which would form 29 of *Lumen Gentium*. 2,055 of 2,152 Fathers voted in favor of the diaconal functions. The admission of deacons of a mature age was accepted by 1,598 out of 2,229 Fathers. On the other hand, the idea of accepting young men without the obligation of celibacy was discarded by 1,364 of the 2,211 voting Fathers. Two modifications to the text had been approved after the discussion in the hall: 1) the request to the Roman Pontiff about the possibility of ordaining married men as deacons and 2) the condition of celibacy for young aspirants.

3. THE TEACHING OF VATICAN II ON THE PD

The Dogmatic Constitution on the Church was promulgated on November 21, 1964. The debate on the diaconate, although it remained poor given the scant theological legacy—according to G. Colombo, "not only does there exist no pre-conciliar theology of the diaconate. But it could not exist, insofar as the magisterium had not had occasion to produce it"[26]—landed on a formulation of the need for the re-establishing the PD which also outlined the coordinates for a subsequent development of diaconal theology. The need was clearly of a practical or pastoral nature; within this pastoral framework, the theological qualities of the diaconal office were drafted, not in a definitional but an expository or descriptive manner.

3.1 *The PD in* Lumen Gentium

The most critical magisterial text of *Lumen Gentium* 29, begins:

> At a lower level of the hierarchy are deacons, upon whom hands are imposed 'not unto the priesthood, but unto a ministry of service.' For strengthened by sacramental grace, in communion with the bishop and his group of priests they serve in the diaconate

---

[26] G. Colombo, *La discussione sul ripristino del diaconato permanente al Concilio Vaticano II. La teologia*, Scuola Cattolica 124 (1996), 646.

of the liturgy, of the word, and of charity to the people of God.

The text then describes the diaconal office, marked by liturgical service through the administration of certain sacraments, by the instruction and exhortation of the people, and finally by charity and assistance.

In the end, the clear will of the majority of the fathers, emerging on a number of occasions in the debate, is clear: the possibility of reinstating the PD in the future since the diaconal offices listed above are "so very necessary to the life of the Church, can be fulfilled only with difficulty in many regions in accordance with the discipline of the Latin Church as it exists today."

Therefore, the diaconate, (necessary to the Church to perform a ministry which would otherwise struggle in the current discipline), can be instituted for "the care of souls." The pastoral note emphasizes a new and fundamental task of the deacon, in symbiosis with the *cura animarum* normally entrusted to the priest. Still, the institution remains at the discretion of the Episcopal Conferences, after the approval of the Pope.

Finally, the text notes that "with the consent of the Roman Pontiff, this diaconate can, in the future, be conferred upon men of more mature age, even upon those living in the married state. It may also be conferred upon suitable young men, for whom the law of celibacy must remain intact   Once again, from all this, the more practical vision which characterizes Vatican II emerges. The stable diaconate was instituted because of the serious difficulties that would arise in fulfilling the diaconal offices under the existing legislation in the Latin Church.

In other words, they desired a stable diaconate, and not as a simple passage to the presbyterate, which would then, according to the needs of the local Churches, have modified the discipline of the Latin Church; and it was not preferred to begin from a more solid doctrine, which would have affirmed the indispensability of a PD giving a new dogmatic momentum and development to a ministry which is indispensable for the ecclesial hierarchy. The debate in the hall did not arrive at a common vision, a sign of the prior uncertainty. Further, the Council did not want to engage its *munus docendi* unnecessarily to remain faithful to its assigned purpose as expressed in the opening address of St. John XXIII. Vatican II instead trusts that the restitution of the diaconate's mark of stability would gradually deepen its intrinsic characteristics. In fact, this modus operandi of the last Ecumenical Assize will engender, in its reception, certain hermeneutical problems in the comprehension of the magisterial texts, and will present the theological need to clarify the correct interpretation of the doctrinal formulas expressing the diaconal ministry. This dogmatic stalemate ultimately does not resolve the great impulse given to the Diakonia. Let us dwell on a few interpretative aspects of *Lumen Gentium* 29.

3.1.1 *"At a lower level"* (*"In gradu inferiori"*)

The Dogmatic Constitution on the Church places the diaconate at a "lower level of the hierarchy." Its inferiority is deduced immediately in relation to the priests, with which the preceding number (n. 28) is concerned. However, relying on the Council of Trent in n. 28a, the text discusses the tripartition of the sacrament of orders without making reference to the inferiority of the diaconate, but an essentially different degree:

> Christ, whom the Father has sanctified and sent into the world, has through His apostles, made their successors, the bishops, partakers of His consecration and His mission. They have legitimately handed on to different individuals in the Church various degrees of participation in this ministry. Thus the divinely established ecclesiastical ministry is exercised on different levels by those who from antiquity have been called bishops, priests and deacons.

The inferiority of the deacon is historically related to the bishop and not directly to the priest; together with the priest, indeed with the entire presbyterate, the deacon serves the bishop as visible head of the Church. The relationship of inferiority is less evident with the priest than with the bishop.[27] The Pauline

---

27 See P. Weber, 91.

letters mention the deacons alongside the bishops (see Phil 1:1; 1Tim 3:8–12). In the *Apostolic Tradition* of Hippolytus, the deacons with the priests who serve the bishop in the liturgical celebrations.[28] This statement, however, must be read in conjunction with the later distinction in the text.

3.1.2 "... not unto the priesthood, but unto a ministry of service"

The formula adopted by the conciliar text to express the difference between the deacon on the one hand, and the bishop and the priest on the other, is apparent. In fact, deacons are ordained not *ad sacerdotium* but *ad ministerium*. However, the preceding number (28a) says that Christ has, through the Apostles, rendered the bishops partakers of his consecration and mission. The bishops have then transmitted this *ministerium* to the Church in various degrees. *Ministry* is not the specific marker of the diaconate but is common to the Sacrament of Orders.

In an official response to a *modus* of two fathers, who claimed the formula used was ambiguous because the priesthood is also a ministry, the Theological Commission interprets a distinction made in the *Statuta Ecclesiae Antiqua*, that "deacons are not ordained to offer the body and blood of the Lord, but the service of charity."[29] In reality, the *Statuta* (the references to the *Statuta* offered in note 110 are also mistaken)[30] says in a general way that the deacon "non ad sacerdotium sed ad ministerium consecratur", to indicate that the deacon is consecrated for the service and ministry of the bishop and priest.[31]

To understand the precise sense of this expression, we must turn to an older source, on which the *Statuta* elaborates. The *Traditio Apostolica* of Hippolytus states that only the bishop

---

28   Hippolytus Romanius, *Traditio Apostolica*, chap. 21–22. See also the *Letters of Ignatius Antiochenus*. The deacons follow and serve the bishop-martyr (Phil. 11:1–2; Smyrn. 10:1). For a synthesis of these Fathers see S. Zardoni, *I diaconi nella Chiesa. Ricerca storica e teologica sul diaconato* (Bologna: 1991), 23–25; 32–34.
29   AS III/8, 101.
30   See A. Mirralles, "*Lo Status Quaestionis della teologia del diaconato permanente*," *Seminarium* 37 (1997), 720.
31   *Statuta Eccl. Ant.* 92 (4) (CChr.SL 148,181): DH 328.

must impose his hands on the deacon for the ordination (in contrast to the ordination of priests in which, in addition to the bishop, priests can also impose their hands), "because he is ordained not unto the priesthood, but unto the service of the bishop, with the task of carrying out his orders."[32] Thus the deacon is assigned only to the service and ministry of the bishop. Zardoni notes:

> the phrase has nothing to do with the exclusion of the deaconate from the scope of what would be called holy orders or ministerial priesthood; "sacerdotium" is the "Eucharistic power", the capacity received by the imposition of hands which renders the bishop and the priest able to celebrate the Eucharistic sacrifice; this is not for the deacon who, according to the *Traditio Apostolica* presents the oblations which will be consecrated by the bishop, and then helps the priests to break the Eucharistic bread.[33]

Hence, the formula adopted by *Lumen Gentium* to define the *proprium* of the diaconate must be read in context. The deacon does not offer the sacrifice of the Mass but serves the bishop or the priest in the Eucharistic celebration. In this regard, the deacon cannot be excluded from the ministerial priesthood in a broad sense, since he represents Christ, head and pastor, through his participation in the Sacrament of Orders, and therefore in the headship of Christ over the Church *suo modo*. To exclude this headship of the deacon, subordinated to the bishop and the presbyterate, is to disregard the ontological distinction, not only of degree, between the ministerial priesthood and the common priesthood of *Lumen Gentium* 10. In any case, exclusion of the mark of headship leaves the deacon out of the ministerial priesthood, placing him incorrectly among the faithful.[34]

---

32 Hippolytus Romanus, *Traditio Apostolica*, c. 8 (Fontes christiani 1, 233) [in the Latin version of the fourth century: *propterea quia non in sacerdotio ordinatur, sed in ministerio episcopi, ut faciat ea quae ab ipso iubentur*].
33 S. Zardoni, cit., pp. 33-34. Translation ours.
34 See M. Hauke, *Das spezifische Profil des Diakonates*, 88–90; Id.,

3.1.3 "... strengthened by sacramental grace"

The council cautiously expresses the diaconate's membership in the sacrament of orders with the formula "strengthened by sacramental grace" (the original text says "*gratia etenim sacramentali roborati*" ; cf. also *Ad Gentes* n. 16). In the hall, the majority of contributions and those most authoritative, relying on the Council of Trent, testified to the sacramentality of the diaconate. Yet, some still denied it or simply expressed some doubt.[35] The *Relatio* of the Doctrinal Commission explains the *caute* in affirming the sacramental nature of the diaconate, albeit founded in Tradition, as a reluctance to give the impression that the council, straying from its pastoral purpose, would condemn those who denied it. Further, the principal biblical text, Acts 6:1–6, according to the exegetes, does not designate in an absolute manner those whom we define as deacons.[36]

J. Beyer, building on ideas that emerged before the Council, expressed the theological reason for opposition to the sacramentality of the diaconate. In his opinion, expressed by G. Philips, the council's prudence in speaking about the depends not so much on its pastoral nature as on a hesitation about the doctrine itself. In fact, even respecting its pastoral purpose, if the doctrine had been mature, the council could have offered a more explicit teaching, without implying *ipso facto* the condemnation of the opposing doctrine.

The ITC (2002) also recognized that Vatican II's prudential manner of expressing the sacramentality of the diaconate was motivated by the "*incertitudo doctrinae.*"

On the other hand, one cannot easily espouse Rahner's thesis either. Since the sacramentality of the diaconate was upheld

---

Diaconato, in G. Calabrese and P. Goyret, O. F. Piazza, *Dizionario di Ecclesiologia* (Rome: 2010), 415–416.
35 See AS II/II, 378. 406. 447s.
36 AS III/I, 260: "*De indole sacramentali diaconatus, statutum est, postulantibus pluribus [...] eam in schemate caute indicare, quia in Traditione et Magisterio fundatur.* Cf. *praeter canonem citatum Tridentini*: Pius XII, Const. Apost. *Sacramentum Ordinis* [DENZ-SCH. 3858 s] [...]. *Ex altera tamen parte cavetur ne Concilium paucos illos recentes auctores, qui de hac re dubia moventur, condemnare videatur.*"

before Vatican II with the minimum value of *"sententia certa et communis,"*[37] Rahner concludes that the tripartition of the Orders into three degrees (episcopate, presbyterate and diaconate), based on their foundation in the Apostolic Church, is of divine right and hence cannot be modified. Yet, the tripartition appears in all its clarity only in the letters of St. Ignatius of Antioch.[38] According to G. Colombo, however, "every uncertainty or hesitation" has been "resolved by the Council, even without a formal definition."[39]

The diaconate certainly forms a part of the Sacrament of Orders (see also LG 28a). Catholics should uphold this claim not only because of the magisterium of the Second Vatican Council, but also because of the doctrinal development in the magisterium after Vatican II,[40] both in the CIC 1983 (canons 1008–1009) and the Catechism of the Catholic Church. Without hesitation, n. 1538 teaches that the ordination of deacons is a sacramental act that bestows the gift of the Holy Spirit so that the recipient is capable of exercising a sacred power, which comes from Christ our Lord himself. The imposition of hands by the bishop and the consecratory prayer are the visible sign of the consecration. The truth of the diaconal *character* or *seal* is then confirmed by n. 1570: "The sacrament of Holy Orders marks [the deacons] with an imprint ('character') which cannot be removed and which configures them to Christ, who made himself the 'deacon' or servant of all."

3.2 The PD in the other documents of Vatican II

The conciliar teaching in the text of LG is the most important one, Vatican II speaks of PD in other documents. There are precisely five direct references to the diaconate in addition to *LG*: 1) according to *Sacrosanctum Concilium* n. 35, at the discretion of the priest the deacon, or some other person authorized by the bishop, can lead the Sunday assembly centered on the Word

---

37 Karl Rahner, *Die Theologie der Erneuerung des Diakonates*, in *Diaconia in Christo*, ed. H. Vorgrimler, 286, note 29.
38 See M. Hauke, *Das spezifische Profil*, 98.
39 G. Colombo, *La discussione sul ripristino del diaconato permanente al Concilio Vaticano II*, 647.
40 For a synthesis see ITC (2002).

of God; 2) the Decree on the Oriental Churches, *Orientalium Ecclesiarum* (n. 17) expresses hope that the PD will be restored in those Churches where it had fallen into disuse; 3) the Decree on Bishops, *Christus Dominus*, (n. 15) teaches that the priests and deacons, in the exercise of their respective power, depend on the bishops, who alone have the fullness of the Sacrament of Orders; 4) *Dei Verbum* n. 25 exhorts the deacons, along with clerics and catechists, to be in continual contact with the Holy Scriptures; 5) Finally, *Ad Gentes*, n. 16 provides one of the most relevant texts on the PD. Like the Constitution *Lumen Gentium*, after urging the re-establishment of the diaconate as a "permanent state" according to the discernment of the Episcopal Conferences, the text proposes to consecrate with the grace of the diaconate — thus to clasp them more securely to the altar — those men "who actually carry out the functions of the deacon's office, either preaching the word of God as catechists, or presiding over scattered Christian communities in the name of the pastor and the bishop, or practicing charity in social or relief work."

Indeed, we ought to praise the missionary sense of this proposal, although it remains equivocal in the affirmation of a 'de facto diaconate' which does not exist. The idea had matured in certain German theological suggestions and experiences, which converged in a magisterial text on the missions, but has fostered the growth of the PD not in third world countries, but in Europe and the United States. If credence were given to this proposal, all the laity occupied in parishes should be promoted clerical status, thus falling into a clericalization of the laity. Zardoni comments:

> the sacrament is not a notarial deed which endorses an already existing reality, but [...] it creates a new reality and a new mode of action. As it is not even conceivable a bishop or a priest 'de facto' to whom it is opportune to add a sacrament so that more effectively, et cetera, thus must the same be said of the diaconate.[41]

While reminding us to interpret the more difficult or problematic passages of the conciliar text correctly, this critical and

---

41 S. Zardoni, 55, note 68.

explanatory note on *Ad Gentes* n. 16 also describes the considerable magisterial and pastoral effort to provide for the permanent restoration of a ministry, which over time had become only a step in accessing the presbyterate.

CONCLUSION

Vatican II lays the foundation—not without new difficulties, among which is the concern for celibacy—for restoring the service proper to the diaconate in the liturgy, the proclamation of the Word of God, and the ministry of charity. It roots the diaconate, not in efficiency-minded or solely pastoral needs, but in the mystery of the Priesthood, whose summit and end is in the Eucharist.

In concluding our *excursus*, the Second Vatican Council wanted to give the *possibility* of restoring the permanent exercise of the diaconate to the local Episcopates, which launched an essential and initial dogmatic development. In synthesis, the council sees the action of the diaconate:[42] 1) as a degree of the *ordained* ministry destined to the service of the bishop and of the priest; 2) which is exercised in three areas that mirror the specific triple *munus* of the Sacrament of Orders (see CIC 1983, can. 1008) (i.e., the Liturgy, the Word, and the exercise of charity), in communion with the bishop and his presbyterate, for the deacon also represents Christ as Head of the Church[43]; and 3) that it is expressed in various tasks or offices in support of the people of God and of its mission in the world, with St. Polycarp's words remaining as an admonition: "Be merciful, diligent, walking according to the truth of the Lord, who became the servant of all."[44]

---

42   For an overall reading, see H. Legrand, *Le diaconat dans sa relation à la théologie de l'Église e des ministères. Réception et devenir du diaconat depuis Vatican II*, in *Diaconat, XXIe siècle*, directed by A. Haquin and P. Weber cit., 13-41.

43   It is also worth noticing a discontinuity between the pastoral *tria munera* (preaching, sanctifying, and leading), and the diaconal trilogy (liturgy, Word, and charity). See A. Borras, *Il diaconato vittima della sua novità?* (Bologna: 2008) (or. *Le diaconat au risque de sa nouveauté*, Bruxelles 2007), 53, even if it is difficult and causing more problems, to deny the deacon of the exercise of the triple *munus* as part of the sacrament of Order. See M. Hauke, *Diaconato*, 416-417.

44   St. Polycarp, *Ad Phil.* 5:2 [cited by LG 29a].

7

The Theological Importance of Humanæ Vitæ
AND ITS PROPHECY FOR OUR TIME

1. *HUMANÆ VITÆ* HAS FACED ACUTE PROBLEMS

Humanæ Vitæ (HV), Pope Paul VI's encyclical on the solemn duty to transmit human life, spoke loud and clear at a troubled historical and cultural moment. On June 25, 1968, Paul VI signed the encyclical, marking the beginning of a major controversy in the Church. Some objected that the Magisterium could not make pronouncements on moral questions beyond the scope of Divine Revelation, for example, on natural moral law, in particular artificial birth control, or contraception. However, HV 4 states that it is beyond dispute, as Paul VI's predecessors teach,

> that Jesus Christ, when He communicated His divine power to Peter and the other Apostles and sent them to teach all nations His commandments, constituted them as the authentic guardians and interpreters of the whole moral law, not only, that is, of the law of the Gospel but also of the natural law. For the natural law, too, declares the will of God, and its faithful observance is necessary for men's eternal salvation.

Some theologians thought that if the principle of totality[1] (a part in relation to a larger whole) was extended to the moral sphere of matrimony, one could claim that the procreative purpose belongs to the entirety of conjugal life and is therefore

---

[1] This principle was formulated with reference to the matter of organ transplants, developed by Pius XII. According to this principle, respect should always be given to oneself and others, as members of the human community regarded as *an organic unity of persons, distinct from one another*.

unaffected by individual acts intended to prevent conception. Individual matrimonial acts would hence be sterilizing in material terms but fertile in formal terms, invoking right intention and separating fertility from an order defined as merely bodily and material, linking it instead to a rational, and hence superior, order. They relied on a morality of effects and consequences combined with convenience, an approach whose grave repercussions continue to this day.

The doctrinal vision presented by HV rests on two principles, which have been abused to support artificial birth control but were explained by Paul VI in the light of Revelation as a whole. These two principles are human love and responsible parenthood.

Human love, which many said was restricted by *Casti Connubii* because it proclaimed marriage's sole purpose was the transmission of life, was upheld as an alternative approach to a static notion of *nature*, focusing instead on the dynamic of the *person* and *communion*. HV 8 teaches that "husband and wife, through that mutual gift of themselves, which is specific and exclusive to them alone, develop that union of two persons in which they perfect one another, cooperating with God in the generation and rearing of new lives."

Responsible parenthood, however, was not defined merely as the predominance of right judgement in the couple's openness to fertility, but also as a decision either to have additional children or "for serious reasons and with due respect to natural law, not to have additional children for either a certain or an indefinite period of time" (HV 10). Further clarifying the limits of responsible parenthood, HV 10 sheds new light on true human love which guides a couple, saying that parents

> are not free to act as they choose in the service of transmitting life, as if it were wholly up to them to decide what is the right course to follow. On the contrary, they are bound to ensure that what they do corresponds to the will of God the Creator. The very nature of marriage and its use makes His will clear, while the constant teaching of the Church spells it out.

The Theological Importance of Humanæ Vitæ

True human love unites parents, making them capable of transmitting the gift of life; the gift of life is, in turn, an expression of human love. This fact is vital in avoiding a division between union and procreation (a binomial which remains indigestible). Paul VI observes in HV 11—a significant magisterial progression from the Second Vatican Council and *Gaudium et Spes* (here authentically interpreted) while holding fast to Pius XI's *Casti Connubii*—that

> the Church [...] in urging men to the observance of the precepts of the natural law, which it interprets by its constant doctrine, teaches that each and every marital act must of necessity retain its intrinsic relationship to the procreation of human life.[2]

With the primary aim of procreation, the truths of love and union are welded together. HV 12 elaborates on the indivisibility of these two aspects:

> This particular doctrine, often expounded by the magisterium of the Church, is based on the inseparable connection, established by God, which man on his own initiative may not break, between the unitive significance and the procreative significance which are both inherent to the marriage act. [...] And if each of these essential qualities, the unitive and the procreative, is preserved, the use of marriage fully retains its sense of true mutual love and its ordination to the supreme responsibility of parenthood to which man is called.

This indivisibility reminds us that the binomial—first expressed by Paul VI and linking *Gaudium et Spes* to *Casti*

---

2   This is the central statement, after making reference to the natural law, whose rule is inserted in the doctrine revealed by God: "[...] *quilibet matrimonii usus ad vitam humanam procreandam per se destinatus permaneat.*" HV here holds fast to *Casti Connubi*: "[...] *quemlibet matrimonii usum, in quo exercendo, actus, de industria hominum, naturali sua vitae procreandae vi destituatur, Dei et naturae legem infringere, et eos qui tale quid commiserint gravis noxae labe commaculari.*" AAS XXII (1930) 560.

Connubii through a reappraisal of the contribution of human and sacramental love to marriage — integrates *union* and *procreation* in the same moral principle, revealing it to be a *procreative union*. Marriage makes a couple one in love with the aim of begetting new life. Hence, the matrimonial union is intended for procreation, and procreation perfects the union in a circular relationship of truth and love: the truth of the union finds its completion in love, which begets new life, and the fertility of love is in turn built on the indissoluble unity of the couple. If this were not the case, love would be false, deceitful. As there is no procreation without union, so there is no union without procreation. Love and fertility go hand in hand and are a reflection of love and unity.

As Stephan Goertz and Caroline Wittin, invoking HV 12, wrote in a recent book of collected essays entitled *Amoris laetitia. Un punto di svolta per la teologia morale? Amoris Laetitia. A turning point for moral theology?*), "contraception is no longer only *contrary to nature*, but also *contrary to love.*"[3]

2. TO WHAT EXTENT DOES HV INTERPRET AND AUTHENTICALLY COMPLETE *GAUDIUM ET SPES* WHILE HOLDING FAST TO *CASTI CONNUBII*?

To begin this brief *excursus*, we must invoke the doctrine of the blessings of marriage, formulated by Augustine, taken up by St. Thomas Aquinas[4] and proclaimed in *Casti Connubii*. "All these — says St. Augustine — are the blessings which make marriage good: procreation, faith and the sacrament."[5] According to Pius XI, these three blessings constitute a splendid compendium of the entire doctrine on Christian marriage. However, *Casti Connubii* affirms that, of the three, procreation has primacy. Marriage is intended by the Creator and elevated by the Redeemer for the procreation of life and the enrichment

---

3   *Amoris laetitia: un punto di svolta per la teologia morale?* eds. S Goertz and C. Witting, (San Paolo: Cinisello Balsamo, 2017), (in German: *Amoris laetitia – Wendepunkt für die Moraltheologie*, Herder, Freiburg im Breisgau 2016), 27.
4   See St. Thomas, *Summa Theologiae*, Supplement, q. 49.
5   St. Augustine, *De bono coniug.*, chap. 24, no. 32.

The Theological Importance of Humanæ Vitæ

of the Holy Church through the begetting of new citizens, that is, the procreation of "fellow citizens of the Saints and members of God's household" (Eph 2:19).

The discourse on the blessings of marriage is joined and intertwined with the discourse on the purposes of marriage (and its properties). The primary end is procreation and the secondary purposes are mutual aid, associated with the blessing of fidelity (*bona fidei*), and the allaying of concupiscence, related to the blessing of indissolubility (*bona sacramenti*). These precepts were initially formulated in the theology of St. Isidore of Seville. The 1917 Code of Canon Law values the expression of the three purposes of marriage, primary and secondary (see Canon 1013, § 1), continuing a long-standing scholastic and controversialist tradition. The relevant theological works endorsed the Canon Law's approach and formulated the discourse on the blessings of marriage on which *Casti Connubii* rests.

However, after *Casti Connubii*, tension developed between a vision of marriage as "an institution given by nature" and a "communion of persons" founded on conjugal love. Some claim this tension arose from the neo-scholastic thinking which underlies Pius XI's encyclical on marriage:

> This mutual moulding of husband and wife, this determined effort to perfect each other, can in a very real sense, as the Roman Catechism teaches [ch. VIII, q. 13], be said to be the chief reason and purpose of matrimony, provided matrimony be looked at not in the restricted sense as instituted for the proper conception and education of the child, but more widely as the blending of life as a whole and the mutual interchange and sharing thereof.[6]

In the writing of *Gaudium et Spes*, two motivations clashed, one defined as *institutionalist* and the other as *personalist*. The former, bolstered by the hierarchy of the purposes of marriage, continuously invoked Holy Scripture, Tradition, and the Magisterium. The latter, on the other hand, rooted in the centrality

---

6 In AAS XXII (1930) 548–549.

of conjugal love, exhorted a broader interpretation of traditional and scriptural works on the three purposes of marriage, seeking the inclusion of love and sexuality in the original plan of the Creator and giving rise to the exigencies of marriage.

Yet, even in *Casti Connubii*, Pius XI refers to the Catechism of the Council of Trent which, even at that date, emphasized love in marriage.[7] For Pius XI, the love in matrimony, which permeates all functions of conjugal life, "holds pride of place in Christian marriage."[8] Indeed, *Casti Connubii* perceives no opposition between nature and the communion of persons, that is, between the natural/sacramental aspect of matrimony and the communion/personalist dimension. This division, arising from an absolutist interpretation of love, was deepened by an unbalanced hermeneutic applied to *Gaudium et Spes* (and the rejection of HV). The interpretation of the Constitution of the Church in the modern world does, in fact, lean toward the personalism of love rather than the hierarchy of the purposes of marriage, placing greater emphasis on the former and neglecting the traditional doctrine of the hierarchy of the purposes of marriage.

In *Gaudium et Spes* 47-52, the imprint of the personalist position of the majority is evident. An entire paragraph (n. 47) is dedicated to human love and, as noted by Goertz and Witting, "the category of 'natural' as an ethical criterion has been consciously dropped."[9] *Gaudium et Spes* 48 affirms that "by their very nature, the institution of matrimony itself and conjugal love are ordained for the procreation and education of children, and find in them their ultimate crown." The same idea is reiterated in paragraph 50. While still emphasizing that the intrinsic purpose (not the primary end, but the purpose deriving from matrimony as an "intimate partnership of life and conjugal love," (GS 48 reiterated

---

7   The Catechism of the Council of Trent (par. 290) gives the following definition of matrimony: "The conjugal union of man and woman, contracted between two qualified persons, which obliges them to live together throughout life."

8   In AAS XXII (1930) 547–548: "[...] *ex coniugali scilicet amore, qui omnia coniugalis vitae officia pervadit et quemdam tenet in christiano coniugio principatum nobilitatis.*"

9   *Amoris laetitia: un punto di svolta per la teologia morale?*, eds. S. Goertz and C. Witting, cit., 25.

in the 1985 Code of Canon Law, Canon 1055, § 1), is procreation, GS no longer mentions that *each single conjugal act is, by its very nature, oriented towards procreation*, as stated in HV, an express reiteration of *Casti Connubii*. The reader is only referred to the doctrine of *Casti Connubii* on the rules on birth control in a footnote to paragraph 51 of *Gaudium et Spes*. Again in note form, GS mentions that problems requiring further and more careful consideration were referred to an ad hoc Commission for the study of the population, the family and the birth rate. Hence, the Conciliar Magisterium offered no concrete solutions on the matter of birth regulation. The study conducted by the Commission was preparatory to Pope Paul VI's Encyclical on human life.

HV fills the void left by *Gaudium et Spes*, condemning contraception and establishing a proper understanding of the value of human love, associated with responsible parenthood and always open to the gift of life. It also harmoniously unites the two inseparable aspects of marriage, the unitive and the procreative (described in paragraph 291 of the Catechism of the Council of Trent as "reasons of the matrimonial union," together with the *remedium concupiscentiae*). Therefore, the link between *Gaudium et Spes* and *Casti Connubii* is restored, the virtualities of the latter are developed, and the truth of conjugal love is planted in the soil of procreation, which is the purpose of each individual act of conjugal love, in cooperation with the design of God. Conjugal love is once again affirmed as *a procreative union*. For this reason, it is expedient, in a discourse on Christian marriage, not to neglect the hierarchical purposes of matrimony, purposes to be continuously embedded in the vital and supreme discourse of procreation, likened to the Creator and the fertile love of Christ for his Bride. The unity of love of husband and wife finds its completion in procreation, even where it is naturally absent because love—from a consistently spiritual and supernatural standpoint—is fertile, or is simply not love.

3. *AMORIS LAETITIA* AS A MEANS OF OVERTAKING HV?

The magisterial teaching of HV provides a clear definition of the immorality of all contraceptive practice:

Similarly excluded is any action which either before, at the moment of, or after sexual intercourse, is specifically intended to prevent procreation — whether as an end or as a means. Neither is it valid to argue, as a justification for sexual intercourse which is deliberately contraceptive, that a lesser evil is to be preferred to a greater one, or that such intercourse would merge with procreative acts of past and future to form a single entity, and so be qualified by exactly the same moral goodness as these." (HV 14)

Paul VI warns against relying on an ethical system based on the "principle of totality" in order to reject the morality of each individual act, thereby rejecting the moral act as such. A morality of the person, understood in opposition to nature, supports the soundness of teleological ethical theories, such as consequentialism and proportionalism, which were condemned by *Veritatis Splendor* but have reappeared in force and are gaining popularity.

HV could be overridden in a context of teleological morality — such as the ethical and moral content of *Amoris Laetitia* (AL), as articulated by its leading interpreters — through the application of a consequentialist or proportionalist morality to the ends chosen, and hence to the intentions of anyone who elects to make a choice rather than refer to the moral object. In a world where human actions are increasingly a blend of good and evil, the only means of adequately assessing the morality of an act is not based on the act itself, the end chosen, which is ultimately ascribed to the person choosing it. Instead, the act should be judged by the desired end, based on a calculation of effects produced or a just proportion between the good achieved and the evil caused. As John Paul II explains in *Veritatis Splendor* 75:

> concrete kinds of behaviour could be described as 'right' or 'wrong', without it being thereby possible to judge as morally 'good' or 'bad' the will of the person choosing them. In this way, an act which, by contradicting a universal negative norm, directly violates goods considered as 'pre-moral' could be qualified as morally acceptable if the intention of the subject is

The Theological Importance of Humanæ Vitæ

focused, in accordance with a 'responsible' assessment of the goods involved in the concrete action, on the moral value judged to be decisive in the situation.

The evaluation of the consequences of the action, based on the proportion between the act and its effects and between the effects themselves, would regard only the pre-moral order. The moral specificity of acts, that is their goodness or evil, would be determined exclusively by the faithfulness of the person to the highest values of charity and prudence, without this faithfulness necessarily being incompatible with choices contrary to certain particular moral precepts.

Let us consider a concrete example. According to "situational ethics," in an adulterous situation (a pre-moral good), if the cohabitants are obliged to remain together for the good of the children, living as husband and wife to safeguard a higher good (the motive being charity and hence a moral good), the moral action would be good because there would be a satisfactory proportionate relationship between the good attained and the wrongful act tolerated. One cannot judge the intention of the agent or the behaviour in itself but only in relation to the circumstances of the case. However, in a situation involving contraception, wherein the moral good of the act in itself is eliminated due to the circumstances (for example the need to safeguard the good of the family as a whole or other children), the moral action would be judged on the basis of a calculation of its effects or the proportionate relationship between the good and bad results. In any event, the morality of the act would no longer pertain to the person or persons choosing this behavior but derive from a calculation based on the end attained. If the end inherent in the act is good (for example, the good of the family), contraception would be morally acceptable. One would consider the agent's intention neutral and hence not open to judgement. Therefore, the objectivity of the moral act *per se* and of the divine precepts, including those which impose prohibitions *semper et pro semper*, is disregarded as futile or immaterial.

Such a morality, which only evaluates the intention and consequences of the act, to the exclusion of the act itself, leads to the acceptance of "intrinsic evils," acts whose object cannot be ordered to God because they radically contradict the good of the person created in His image and violate what St. Paul says in his letter to the Romans (3:8): "It is not licit to do evil that good may come of it."[10]

A closer examination of AL reveals two paragraphs that lend themselves to interpretation in this direction. AL 80, affirms that:

> no genital act of husband and wife can refuse this [generative] meaning [here reference to HV 11–12 is made], even when for various reasons it may not always in fact beget a new life.

As noted by Goertz and Witting, "this is surely an ambiguous assertion because, from a 'not licit,' one proceeds to a 'not being able.' Is fertility of love to be understood here as transcending actual procreation?"[11] The reasons for refusal are not identified or even qualified as "grave," but are mere reasons, ultimately ascribable to the supreme reason of love, which, in a more general interpretation, precedes or is implicit in procreation. AL 82 further paves the way for a "shift in moral paradigm," when, quoting the *Relatio Synodi*, it states that:

---

10 *Veritatis Splendor* 79 teaches: "One must therefore reject the thesis, characteristic of teleological and proportionalist theories, which holds that it is impossible to qualify as morally evil according to its species – its 'object' — the deliberate choice of certain kinds of behaviour or specific acts, *apart* from a consideration of the intention for which the choice is made or the totality of the foreseeable consequences of that act for all persons concerned." Paragraph 81 adds: "In teaching the existence of intrinsically evil acts, the Church accepts the teaching of Sacred Scripture. The Apostle Paul emphatically states: 'Do not be deceived: neither the immoral, nor idolaters, nor adulterers, nor sexual perverts, nor thieves, nor the greedy, nor drunkards, nor revilers, nor robbers will inherit the Kingdom of God' (1 Cor 6:9–10)." Lastly, *Veritatis Splendor* 80 quotes HV 14, in so doing ratifying its magisterial authority on matter of intrinsic evil acts with direct reference to contraception. Therefore, the Encyclical *Veritatis Splendor*, by reiterating the teaching of HV (in the light of the magisterial tradition as a whole) and invoking it as an authority on this matter, allows us to hold HV to be *definitive magisterial teaching* on contraception.

11 *Amoris laetitia: un punto di svolta per la teologia morale?*, eds. S. Goertz and C. Witting, cit. 57.

The Theological Importance of Humanæ Vitæ

We need to rediscover the message of the Encyclical *Humanæ Vitæ* of Blessed Pope Paul VI, which highlights the need to respect the dignity of the person in morally assessing methods of regulating birth....

In fact, HV never refers to the dignity of the person in an assessment of birth control methods; instead, by maintaining conjugal morality in its entirety and consistently denouncing contraception as directly contrary to the unitive and procreative aspect of marriage, the Church is defending the dignity of husband and wife (see HV 18). However, quoting *Gaudium et Spes* 50 in AL 222, Pope Francis underlines the *dignity* of the spouses, inviting them to form a right judgement before God about bringing children into the world. He adds that the use of natural methods of birth control should be encouraged.

An influential moral theologian, Eberhard Schockenhoff[12] (theological adviser to several German prelates), perceives in AL a "Paradigmenwechsel," a "paradigm shift" (which has also attracted many followers in Italy). He claims that if we follow the exhortation of Pope Francis on love in the family, we would be "downplaying the sexuality" affirmed in recent centuries. The title of AL invites us to gaze from on high at the playfulness, passion and ecstasy of love. According to Schockenhoff, AL 82 is particularly expressive of this shift in moral perspective. In his opinion, the text should be read in light of Pope Francis's skeptical observations on the overestimation of a deductive moral theory, which, from general principles, aims to solve all possible ethical issus. Schockenhoff senses behind this text "a tendency to relativize the teaching hitherto upheld of the absolute moral censure of artificial birth control."

In other words, according to this German theologian, AL paves the way for an overhaul of the moral doctrine on contraception by advocating a personalistic morality rather than the existing

---

12   See his essay *Traditionsbruch oder notwendige Weiterbildung. Zwei Lesarten des Nachsynodalen Schreibens "Amoris Laetitia,"* in "Stimme der Zeit" 3 (2017) 147–158. A digital version is available: www.stimmen-derzeit.de/zeitschrift/archiv/beitrag_details?k_beitrag=4797115&k_produkt=None. We will refer to this essay in its digital version.

neo-scholastic or essentialist morality. Is this the guiding idea behind the new Commission, established to monitor the historical progress of HV, thereby identify possible links between this document and *Gaudium et Spes* instead of *Casti Connubii*? Are we to be confronted once more with the invocation of an absolute Conciliar Magisterium, contrary to the Church's unwavering tradition and developed homogenously and definitively in its earliest beginnings by the Pontifical Magisterium of the last fifty years?

Furthermore, as Schockenhoff points out, this would be a propitious moment to set aside a morality based upon the neo-scholastic moral act derived from the ethics of St. Thomas Aquinas. Rather than a morality of acts (and their object), we would move, as in AL, to a morality of the person. This new paradigm would present an easy solution to the problem of remarried divorced persons. If we no longer need to judge consciences, then we must ask whether the life shared by remarried divorced persons is loved in its moral value. If what matters is the communion and personalism aspect, then, in the German theologian's view, even a civil union should be seen as a bond and an entirely personal community of life. Reference to 'rupture' of the abandoned partner would be simply absurd. This is the extreme conclusion results from the "paradigm shift" and would lead to substantial repercussions on life and procreation within marriage. The love formerly proclaimed would be trampled.

CONCLUSION

There is a great effort to generate an irreversible turnaround in moral theology, encouraged by AL. Thus, many suggest reading AL in light of *Gaudium et Spes* to disregard the (neo-scholastic and jusnaturalistic) norms solidified in HV, which are organically linked to *Casti Connubii* and the traditional moral doctrine on marriage. They would neglect an ethic based on the law or the norm in favor of an ethic of the person, love, or responsibility. The moment of this disregard is essential and programmatic. It is fed by characteristic prolixity, transformed into a pedagogical method. In the opinion of another German theologian, H. K. Pottmeyer, prolixity (or verbosity) is instrumental to the desired transition: "Through persuasive language, it is intended to obtain support for a new beginning, while at the same time demonstrating continuity."[13]

We should therefore focus increasingly on an analysis of the language employed and its proper usage in theology. This reckless shift in paradigm threatens not only the morality of marriage but morality itself, which could be reduced to good intentions. However, we must hold firm so that our "Yes" means "Yes" and our "No" means "No." Whatever goes beyond this comes from evil (cf. Mt 5:37).

---

13   H. J. Pottmeyer, "Von einer neuen Phase der Rezeption des Vaticanum II. Zwanzig Jahre Hermeneutick des Konzils," in *Die Rezeption des Zweiten Vatikanischen Konzils*, eds. H. J. Pottmeyer, G. Alberigo, and J. P. Jossua (Düsseldorf 1986), 48. cit. in *Amoris laetitia: un punto di svolta per la teologia morale?*, eds. S. Goertz and C. Witting, 56.

8

To the Root of Today's Church Crises:
A THEOLOGICAL COLLAPSE

Holy Mother Church is facing a crisis unprecedented in her entire history. Abuses of all kinds, especially in the sexual sphere, have always existed among the clergy. The current epidemic, however, is atypical because of the intersection of a moral crisis and a doctrinal one, whose roots are deeper than the simple misbehaviour of some members of the hierarchy and clergy. We must beyond the surface level. Doctrinal confusion begets moral disorder, and vice versa; sexual abuses have prospered under the cover of complacency for so many years and to such an extent that they have silently turned the doctrine of sexual morality into an anachronistic story.

As Bishop Egan of Portsmouth, UK, said, this crisis exists on three levels: "first, the alleged catalogue of sins and crimes against the young by members of the clergy; secondly, the homosexual circles centered around Cardinal McCarrick, but present in other areas across the Church, too; and then, thirdly, the mishandling and cover-up of all this by the hierarchy up to the highest circles."

How far have we to go to identify the roots of this crisis? There are essentially two moral causes; one is remotely linked with the problem afflicting the Church today, the other proximately.

The first cause is rooted in the opposition within the Church to the encyclical *Humanæ Vitæ*. By objecting to the indissoluble covenant between the unitive and procreative principles of marriage, they paved the way for tolerating any form of union, justifying them in the name of love. Love would be valued before and above the fixity of nature. Contraception would be counted as a morally legitimate means to safeguard the priority of man's responsibility over God's natural and divine law. The scenario that unfolded was quite different. Since procreation was no longer the first and highest blessing of marriage, it was not only split from love, but, conversely, love was divorced from procreation. Now, procreation without union is justified as the logical conclusion of love without procreation. A sterile love, isolated from its natural and sacramental context, was forcefully pushed onto society and the Church.

Love's identity is at stake. As recently pointed out by Bishop Doran, the chair of the Irish Bishops' Committee for Bioethics, there is a "direct connection between the 'contraceptive mentality' and the surprisingly high number of people who seem ready to redefine marriage today as a relationship between two people without distinction as to sex." He added that if the act of love can be separated from its procreative purpose, "then it is also pretty difficult to explain why marriage needs to be between a man and a woman." Today's crisis in the Church is, on the one hand, the manifestation of a sexual identity crisis, an ideological rebellion against a Magisterium anchored in a perennial moral tradition; and on the other, the incapacity to address the real problem, namely, homosexuality and homosexual circles among the clergy. More than 80% of known sexual abuses committed by clergy are not cases of paedophilia but pederasty. The conviction that any form of love must be accepted has become more common since the ban on contraception was lifted, even without changing dogmatic formulas. The very essence of modernism consists in changing the theory with the praxis by familiarizing people with the customs accepted by the majority.

Humanæ Vitæ sparked an unprecedented protest within the Church. *The Schism of '68* describes, among other things, how Catholics were campaigning for a sexual aggiornamento. 'Aggiornamento' was one of the keys to unlocking Vatican II and its documents. Cardinals, bishops, and episcopates took an active role in this rebellion. The primate of Belgium, Cardinal Leo Joseph Suenens, after the encyclical's publication, convinced the whole Belgian Episcopate to publish a declaration in opposition to *Humanæ Vitæ*, supposedly in the name of freedom of conscience. This declaration, together with another formulated by the German Episcopate, served as a template for later protests. Cardinal Heenan of Westminster described the release of Pope Paul VI's encyclical on the transmission of life as "the greatest shock since the Reformation." Cardinal Alfrink, together with nine other Dutch bishops, even voted in favour of the *Independence Declaration*, which invited the people of God to reject the ban on contraception.

In England, more than fifty priests drew up a letter of protest, published in *The Times of London*. One of these men, Michael Winter, claimed that his decision to leave the priesthood was "sparked by the crisis over *Humanæ Vitæ*." Winter later married, and, in 1985, authored *Whatever Happened to Vatican II?* in an attempt to resurrect the council's teaching from what he perceived as its burial by the authorities in Rome. Perhaps he thought that the root of contraception, which he saw as the supremacy of love, was implanted in Vatican II's teaching. Winter is also a founding member of the Movement for a Married Clergy. What is truly astonishing—and Winter is not the only case—is the drama the clergy experienced when, in their words, the burden of the ban on contraception was laid on the shoulders of the laity. How could they really understand such a pain—if there was any?

There is another point to consider. If an "official" protest against *Humanæ Vitæ*, led by cardinals and bishops, was deemed legitimate because it harmonized with the ideology of the moment—at this time, the '68 movement was intent on subverting Christian morality in the name of free sex—then it is hard to see why an "official" mentality that justifies homosexuality, and all kinds of sexual unions, within the clergy could not also take over and even become the majority view. The cover-up culture, which today seems so pervasive among episcopacies and the clergy, arises from this.

"If the matter is before the bar of conscience," as Tom Burns commented in *The Tablet* on August 3, 1968 (the same editorial was republished on July 28, 2018), any conscience can reject the bar as such. A conscience that lacks prior enlightenment by the truth is like a ship buffeted by the sea. It capsizes. *Conscience alone*—conscience without the truth—is no conscience at all.

It has to be educated to pursue good and reject evil. It is no mystery that those working to ultimately bury HV rejoice at the promulgation of *Amoris Laetitia*, as if some gap of love in the Church's teaching has finally been filled. Some attempt to subvert HV with *Amoris Laetitia* by tying Pope Francis's teaching on love in the family directly with *Gaudium et Spes*, ignoring HV and *Casti Connubii*. The temptation to isolate Vatican II from the whole Tradition of the Church is still strong. As "conscience alone" cannot stand, neither can a single document of the Magisterium (either *Gaudium et Spes* or *Amoris Laetitia*); no document can be read in the light of itself but only in light of the whole Tradition of the Church.

After an initial vocal rebellion, silence on the doctrine reigned. And so, we come to the proximate root of this scandal: the cover-up of the doctrine of sin. The word *sin* began to disappear from pulpits in the aftermath of Vatican II. Sin—separation from God and an offence against Him, a turning away from God and a fixation on creatures—was ignored. The extraordinary gap left by the doctrine of sin was filled with psychological assessments of a multifaceted condition of weakness in man. Spiritual theology was replaced with the writings of Freud and Jung, the true masters in many seminaries. Sin faded into irrelevance while self-esteem and triumph over taboos, especially in the sexual sphere, became the new ecclesial passwords.

On the other hand, a new theology of mercy, promoted by Cardinal Kasper, helped to reframe God's mercy as an intrinsic attribute of his divine essence (if so, does God grant divine forgiveness to Himself, since mercy requires repentance and forgiveness?). This interpretation overthrows the punishment of justice by turning it into an always-forgiving love. Under this new definition, does the eternal punishment in hell play any role? Mercy is transformed into a theological surrogate to cover (up) sin, ignore it, and take it under the mantle of forgiveness. This understanding of mercy echoes Luther's idea about justification.

It would be interesting to ask the clergy who commit such horrible crimes what they think of sin. St. Paul's teaching—"... they that are Christ's have crucified their flesh, with the vices and concupiscences" (Gal 5:24)—might be discounted as old-fashion morality, not because Scripture is wrong or uninspired but because such a claim is seen as anachronistic or outmoded in our modern society. The spirit of the world—often mixed with a supposed spirit of the council—has been allowed to suffocate the true doctrine of faith and morals.

Is clericalism also the root of the present sexual abuse crisis? Pope Francis has repeatedly said so. Certainly, some clergy wield their power for the sexual enslavement of seminarians and men in formation. However, clericalism cannot explain the predation of generations of seminarians if homosexuality plays no role at all. That would be like saying that a drinker is always drunk, not because he has an addiction to drink, but because he has money and can buy all the alcohol he likes. Clericalism cannot be the only source of the problem because it takes on another form—more subtle and often ignored—that is far worse: the perversion of sound doctrine. The clergy can often see themselves as the owners of the Gospel, with the license to diverge from the precepts of God and the Church and align themselves with the current fashionable theology. When one ceases to adhere to the right doctrine of the Church, one can easily fall into the pit of self-amusement and sin. Conversely, a life of sin without God's sanctifying grace is the best ally to manipulate doctrine. Faith and morals always go together.

The very root of this grievous scandal is modernism, which has already become postmodernism. No longer content to change dogmatic formulas with the flow of time, we have graduated to ignore them completely. Like a great book on a dusty shelf, doctrine has no influence on our daily life. There must be no doubt about the vastness of this crisis and the need to take action to root out the present evil. However, any action will be far from effective if we do not first return to the truth of love and realize that a contraceptive mentality has only created a severe demographic winter and a culture of death. Contraception is sterile love that generates the possibility of a love outside its context, beyond itself, and immature. A dead love, producing visible repercussions in the form of sexual abuse and clerical scandals, now threatens the Church. The mentality of the world has violently impacted the life of the Church. We must recultivate the habit of calling things by their name. Sin is still sin. If we lack the strength to denounce it, that is a sign that sin has prevailed. If we do call sin by its name, then we can begin to root it out.

9

The Uneasy Path from Gaudium et Spes to Humanæ Vitæ

THE GRAVE MORAL CRISIS OF SEXUAL abuses flooding the Church is rooted deeper than the misbehaviour of some priests and prelates. Certainly, it is not simply an expression of the human weakness that the youth would understand better than any other, since they themselves fall and get back up, as recently insinuated by Cardinal Baldisseri in a press conference for the presentation of the Youth Synod (October 1, 2018). Will the young victims of numerous clerical predators understand this weakness? The root of the problem is both dogmatic and moral. It begins with the rejection of Christ's doctrine on human love and sexuality. As I said in the previous essay, this doctrine was "officially" rebuffed with a public rebellion against *Humanæ Vitæ* within the Church. Questioning the indissoluble bond between conjugal love and procreation opened the door to justify any possible union. However, we cannot fully understand the storm that arose in the Church without examining the initial moment of the "official" disagreement about the ban on contraception, which then escalated to a public rebellion against Paul VI. The protest caught fire publicly, but the fire was already smouldering beneath the ashes. We must look behind the scenes of Vatican II to discover the beginning of the animosity. Two key figures dominate: Cardinal Leo Joseph Suenens, the primate of Belgium; and Schema XIII that later became the Pastoral Constitution *Gaudium et Spes*.

Suenens calls himself in his *Mémoires* (a 69-page text dictated by the Belgian Cardinal immediately after the council that contains his memoirs and constitutes documents 2784 and 2785 of the "Suenens Archive") as "the father, the initiator" of *Gaudium et Spes*. He also writes that he was not "extremely enthusiastic" about it, since Paul VI sent four *modi*, on November 23, 1965, that reaffirmed the classical doctrine of the Church on matrimony by modifying paragraphs 51, 54, and 55 of the drafted text. These

The Symphony of Truth

modi, among others, clarified Church doctrine on birth control, holding fast to *Casti Connubii*, which the Pope wanted to be explicitly quoted. Before the *modi*, Paul VI had asked Suenens to prepare a possible declaration open to birth control, in line with the Belgian primate's own position. Suenens reacted strongly to the denial of that pontifical declaration. He wanted to campaign among the council fathers to convince them to vote against the new text. He only decided to vote placet after Msgr. Prignon assured him that Msgr. Heuschen and Prof. Heylen had made those *modi* inoffensive and that the question on birth control was pending in the conciliar text.

Suenens supported Schema XIII because he hoped to see the Church's position on birth control modified in the chapter entitled *De Matrimonio*. On May 7, 1964, Suenens launched a *baillon d'essai* at a press conference in Boston, saying: "Medical research is coming very close to finding a pill which will make it very easy for married couples to plan their families without violating the teachings of the Church." As Werner Wan Laer observed, thanks to Cardinal Suenens, the chapter on matrimony in *Gaudium et Spes* remains one of the Vatican II texts most open to interpretation.

Moreover, Suenens, whom Paul VI appointed as moderator of the council with three other cardinals (Agagianian, Döpfner and Lercaro), was able to introduce four questions in the Council hall in relation to the sacramentality and collegiality of the episcopate and the reintroduction of the permanent diaconate. Without the support of Paul VI, who was hesitant, and against the will of Ottaviani and Pericle Felici (Council Secretary), the moderators, particularly Suenens, proposed to an "indicative ballot" on the four questions. The ballot, scheduled for October 17, 1963, was known to the press and publicized by *Avvenire d'Italia*. Paul VI postponed the ballot and ordered all 3000 voting cards, whose printing was commissioned by Cardinal Lercaro, burned. At this point, the long-standing friendship between the Belgian primate and the Pope started to crack, eventually leading Suenens to rebuke Paul VI for not handling the publication of his encyclicals *Sacerdotalis Caelibatus* (1967) and *Humanæ Vitæ* (1968) in a collegial manner.

Paul VI did not want the council to debate birth control. Suenens tells in his *Mémoires* that Cardinal Agagianian, who chaired the current council session, had prepared a text that told the fathers to avoid discussion of that topic. Suenens modified the text to say: "We will discuss this subject, but only in reference to the first principles, without entering into details." Paul VI became irate with Suenens and — as related by the latter — told him that he had lost his credibility with the council bishops. However, Suenens was proud of his actions. One of his colleagues, the rector of the Belgian College, Fr. Aeber Prignon (1919–2000), told him: "You opened the future." Fr. Prignon was correct; Suenens actions have led us to a bleak future, with numerous problems for the world, but especially for the Church.

Suenens entrusted his hope for suitable successive hermeneutics of *Gaudium et Spes* in the document's optimistic tenor, with its descriptive rather than assertive sentences. However, many were dissatisfied with Schema XIII (formerly XVII), which later became *Gaudium et Spes*, but not for the same reason as Suenens. Despite the document's well-publicized launch, according to Fr. Henri de Lubac, "the outcome was mediocre; no doctrinal coherence, and more, no Christian strength. Many bishops see this, and say this in private and in public, but there is no way to fully remedy it; it is too late." Even more grievous, Msgr. Blanchet's critique of *Gaudium et* Spes, highlighted by Cardinal Siri, says that there was "an excess of optimism, with no allusion to what is however a feature of our time: the diminishing of the sense of sin."

Suenens appealed to collegiality, a theme strongly debated in the council and advanced by Cardinal Parente, who supported the claims of the "collegials." However, because collegiality itself needed to be repaired, the *Nota Praevia* was added to *Lumen Gentium*. Suenens stubbornly alleged a lack of collegiality in the making of *Humanæ Vitæ*. He also firmly believed that the open teaching of *Gaudium et Spes* would facilitate a future magisterial statement in support of birth control. While this never came to fruition, it is the key to understanding Suenens's rebellion against the Magisterium of Paul VI. This rebellion is symbolic; it shows the dead end of the divorce between one's ideas and the magisterium of the Church.

The post-conciliar confusion and the rebellion against *Humanæ Vitæ* are tied — albeit indirectly — to the magisterial uncertainty of Vatican II, especially in *Gaudium et Spes*. One cannot simply blame the contrasting hermeneutics during the receptive phase of the council. The council itself, with its doctrinal ambiguity on various points, created the hermeneutical problem. From the beginning of the council, the fathers and their theologians faced such a problem. The dispute between Paul VI and the Theological Commission over the constitutive value of Apostolic Tradition is just one example; Paul VI reaffirmed Apostolic Tradition with the previous Magisterium, but the majority of expert theologians and the fathers omitted it for the sake of "ecumenism." The recent attempt to link *Amoris Laetitia* to *Gaudium et Spes* further proves that opposition to *Humanæ Vitæ* is rooted in the pastoral constitution of Vatican II. Those behind the attempt hope to overcome Paul VI's encyclical letter on life by reclaiming the conciliar magisterium on conjugal love in the family, introducing an alleged "dignity of the person" in morally assessing methods of regulating birth (cf. AL 82), and justifying *de facto* the *more uxorio* marital intercourse.

There is another consequence. The synod of bishops under Francis now has a new status. The issues for discussion are raised by man — by the people, specifically the youth. The Church "listens" and does not teach. The synod teaching, if approved by the Supreme Pontiff, will be part of his ordinary Magisterium — a tangible idea of "the Church from below," a magisterium continuously developing as an open construction site (or a "field hospital"), and a superimposition of roles between lay people and the ministerial priesthood. Does this new "synod paradigm" promote the conciliar collegiality stopped by the *Nota Praevia* but vehemently advanced by Suenens with a vision of a Church *in fieri*, where the (collegial) consent of the majority is preponderant? If so, Vatican II, on the one hand, would rise once again to a conciliar paradigm and, on the other, would also be used as a smokescreen for a new opposition in the Church to Her perennial magisterium. Such a magisterial break and its supposed new beginning are like anesthetics for the conscience; they are used to exorcise the ghosts of gloomy and prohibitive morals. This confirms that the final root of today's moral crisis is found in the attempt to subvert correct doctrine in the name of conciliar plurality. Unending hermeneutics does not solve any problem but creates new and grievous ones.

10

A 'Sacerdotal People of God':
A LOOK AT THE PRIESTHOOD OF MARY AND HER VICTIMHOOD AS CO-REDEMPTRIX

1. THE CHURCH AS A SACERDOTAL PEOPLE OF GOD

The Church is the House of God (see 1 Tim 3:15) composed of members regenerated to divine grace through Baptism. All together these members of the Church constitute a sacerdotal people of God, among which we can distinguish, from its origin, a common priesthood and a ministerial priesthood. The whole body is made up of people who are members in Christ and as living stones help to edify the Church herself, who is the Temple of God (see 1 Pt 2:5). The people are set apart to build up a spiritual temple, a new holy nation. The words of St. Peter express this mystery: "But you are a chosen race, a kingdom of priests, a holy nation, a people to be a personal possession to sing the praises of God who called you out of the darkness into his wonderful light" (1 Pt 2:9).

Therefore, all the baptized, by regeneration and the anointing of the Holy Spirit, are consecrated as a holy priesthood. Through their Christian works, they are able to offer spiritual sacrifices to God and to proclaim the power of the Resurrection of Christ, bearing witness to Him. All Christians are called to transform every activity into a spiritual offering (prayers and sacrifices), to God, and to offer themselves as a living sacrifice, holy and pleasing to the Lord (see Rm 12:1).

This sacerdotal nation, the Church of Christ, is permeated from her origin by the presence of the twelve Apostles, who are the generative principle of the sacred Hierarchy and the new People of God. Christ established the Church on the foundation stone of St. Peter's faith and, granting the Apostles his same authority, he sent them to fulfil his own ministry, to gather from the four winds all people called to enter the Church (see Mt 28: 16-20). This apostolic ministry sanctifies the people, making them acceptable to God as an offering purified by the Holy Spirit (see Rom 15:16).

Since her founding, the Church has contemplated two forms of priesthood: a common priesthood of all the faithful, and a ministerial one, that of the Apostles and of their successors. The two forms of priesthood differ essentially from one another. They do not originate from one another, but both draw their nature from Christ, the High Priest, who extends his salvific power in the Church through the ministerial priesthood. The ordained ministry is responsible for infallibly assuring the presence of Christ, the Head and Spouse of the Church, so that the sacerdotal people of God might always offer worship and spiritual sacrifice as a gift of the Bride. Christ is the groom and the ordained minister as well. The faithful are part of the Church as body and bride.

Lumen Gentium, Vatican II's Dogmatic Constitution on the Church, in explaining the ontological difference between the two forms of priesthood and what concerns their relationship, says:

> Though they differ from one another in essence and not only in degree, the common priesthood of the faithful and the ministerial or hierarchical priesthood are nonetheless interrelated: each of them in its own special way is a participation in the one priesthood of Christ. The ministerial priest, by the sacred power he enjoys, teaches and rules the priestly people; acting in the person of Christ, he makes present the Eucharistic sacrifice, and offers it to God in the name of all the people. But the faithful, in virtue of their royal priesthood, join in the offering of the Eucharist. They likewise exercise that priesthood in receiving the sacraments, in prayer and thanksgiving, in the witness of a holy life, and by self-denial and active charity.

The ministerial priesthood, as a sacramental mediation between Christ and the people, enables the faithful, above all, to actively participate in the offering of the Eucharist during

Holy Mass. The priest gives all the baptized the grace of uniting themselves with the present on the altar by offering the Holy Sacrifice of the Mass and distributing the Holy Bread of Life. He also enables them to participate in the offering of that sacrifice and themselves to God. For this reason, the priest, at the offertory of the Mass, turns towards the people and says: "Pray brethren that my sacrifice and yours may be acceptable to God." Christ is the one sacrifice offered by the priest with the prayer and the lay contribution of the faithful. The faithful offer God their own body and soul in union with the Holy Sacrifice of the Mass to be truly one with Christ. In summary, salvation comes from Christ to the people of God through the ministerial priesthood of the Apostles and priests; conversely, all prayers and gifts accepted by God rise to Christ from the Church through the ministry of the Apostles and priests.

2. THE PRIESTHOOD OF CHRIST

The Letter to the Hebrews calls Christ "the supreme high priest." His priesthood is eternal and new. It does not come from the line of the Levites and it is not according to the priesthood of Aaron, but God the Father entrusted the priestly ministry to Christ when the Son was begotten according to human flesh and became man. Christ became man to suffer and die for us, to offer the supreme sacrifice for our salvation. As Paul says in the Letter to the Hebrews:

> Since in Jesus, the Son of God, we have the supreme high priest who has gone through to the highest heaven we must never let go of the faith that we have professed. For it is not as if we had a high priest who was incapable of feeling our weaknesses with us; but we have one who has been tempted in every way that we are, though he is without sin. (4:14-16)

Jesus in his human nature is the priest immolated for us on the altar of the Cross. On the Cross, Christ offers the sacrifice of his body and blood, anticipated and perpetuated by the offering of the Holy Eucharist on Maundy Thursday and at every Holy

Mass. Christ is the priest according to the emblematic figure of Melchizedek (see Heb 7). He "offered himself as the perfect sacrifice to God through the eternal Spirit", and for that "He brings a new covenant, as the mediator" (Heb 9:14-15). This covenant is eternal, and it is sealed with Christ's precious Blood, "the Blood of the new and eternal covenant," as the priest repeats at every Holy Mass, where Christ acts as the only High Priest.

Upon reflection, we arrive at a definition of Christ's priesthood: a 'sacrificial mediation' of the incarnate Word to realize a 'sacrifice of communion' for those who will be saved; a communion with God and among men. Christ offers himself to rescue sinners. His oblation—his own Body and Blood—reconciles God with mankind and mankind with God. Priesthood is essentially a mediation that inaugurates a new communion in Christ between God and his holy priestly people. The ordained priest is a representation of Christ as Head of this priestly people. He enables them to be in communion with God by acting in the person of Christ in the so-called 'ascendant mediation' (expiation and satisfaction offered to God) and to receive grace and supernatural life in the so called 'descendant mediation' (from God to us).

3. WHERE CAN WE PLACE OUR LADY?[1]

The whole Church shares in Christ's priesthood, each member sharing in one of the two forms. The only source of priesthood is Christ. But how does Our Lady participate in Christ's Priesthood? To answer this question we must understand how she shares in Christ's salvific mission. She has not been ordained a priest; only the twelve Apostles and their successors (bishops and priests) were ordained. Thus, Mary must be a member of the Church's universal priesthood, which is rooted in the sacraments of baptism and confirmation.

Post-Vatican II, many theologians place the Blessed Virgin among the baptized, although they grant her primacy as a type of

---

[1] I have dedicated to this topic my doctoral thesis. See S. M. Lanzetta, *Il sacerdozio di Maria nella teologica cattolica del XX secolo. Analisi storico-teologica* (Frigento: Casa Mariana Editrice, 2006).

A 'Sacerdotal People of God'

the common priesthood. Our Lady is the "type of the sacerdotal people of God." The late mariologist Stefano de Fiores held this position. He re-evaluated an ancient title given to Mary, *Virgo Sacerdos*, interpreting it to refer to the common priesthood of Mary, eminently exercised on account of her sublime prerogative as the Mother and Helpmate of Christ. Thus, we turn to the main question of this paper: is it satisfactory to view Our Lady as a type of the sacerdotal people of God? Is she a common member of the People of God, even if an eminent one? Or can we say something more?

3.1 Type or figure

Our Lady is indeed a type but of the entire Church, i.e. the mystical body of Christ, and she is Mother of the whole Body. The word 'type' means 'figure' and is characterized by three fundamental features: 1) a concrete representation of an invisible and spiritual reality (in our context, the baptismal priesthood, *sacerdotium*); 2) an internal bond between the figure and the reality; 3) a moral exemplarity drawing from the representation. Mary is the perfect figure of the Church because she unites in her person those properties which also enrich the Church, that is, great faith, charity, and union with Christ. Her divine maternity and her perpetual virginity are a sublime figure of the Church as virgin and mother (see LG 63-64). Moreover, Our Lady, as a type of the Church, is already that perfection which the Church is invited to reach in all her members. Mary is enthroned in Heaven and is already and definitively what the Church is called to become progressively till the end of time. Mary is a type or figure of the Church because, in her immaculate person, she prefigures the Church as Bride of Christ and Woman. Our Blessed Mother stands before the Church as a pattern of perfection.

The reasons expressed above convince some authors that the term 'type' is imperfectly applied to Mary, because the figure, Mary, is greater than the reality, the Church (or the common priesthood, if we consider Mary as a type of the sacerdotal people of God). For this reason, some authors prefer to speak of Mary as 'archetype,' that is, the first and the original type or figure.

3.2 Mother of the Church

The Blessed Virgin is Mother of the Church. She is Mother of the whole body, of the Head and the members, generated when she said 'Yes' at the Annunciation on behalf of mankind, echoing the 'Yes' of the Saviour: "Here I am Lord. I come to do your will" (Ps 39:7-9 and Heb. 10:5-7). Our Lady, as the Woman-Mother, suffered with Christ on Calvary to bring God's children to supernatural life by uniting herself to the sacrifice of Christ and offering it uniquely as mother and 'spouse' of Christ. She is 'spouse' of her Son only because she is intimately united with him, literally one flesh with him, in saving all mankind. On Calvary, the unique cooperation of Mary in Redemption, more accurately *Co-Redemption*, reaches its apex. This cooperation covers all her life, spent in intimate union with Christ. Vatican II synthesizes it in this way:

> Predestined from eternity by that decree of divine providence which determined the incarnation of the Word to be the Mother of God, the Blessed Virgin was on this earth the virgin Mother of the Redeemer, and above all others and in a singular way the generous associate and humble handmaid of the Lord. She conceived, brought forth and nourished Christ. She presented Him to the Father in the temple, and was united with Him by compassion as He died on the Cross. In this singular way she cooperated by her obedience, faith, hope and burning charity in the work of the Saviour in giving back supernatural life to souls. Wherefore she is our mother in the order of grace (LG 61).

3.3 The sacrifice of Mary

The Blessed Virgin Mary is the only one who cooperated actively and directly with Christ during his earthly life in accomplishing God's plan of salvation. She had a unique role with Christ in the final offering of the divine sacrifice of our Redemption. Calvary is of the greatest importance. We have been delivered from our sins by the sacrifice of Christ offered on the Cross.

Since Our Lady is present at the foot of the Cross as *Alma Socia Christi*, as Pius XII says, that is, as intimate Helpmate of Christ, then she truly contributes by her immaculate and maternal action to our deliverance from sin. With Christ, she offers the sacrifice of salvation. As helpmate and mother, she offers Christ, and in Christ she offers herself. The supreme sacrifice offered by Christ on Calvary is the summit of Christ's eternal priesthood, and it helps us discern more about Mary's unique sharing in the priesthood of Christ. On Golgotha, Our Lady offered her own sacrifice, which is singular and unique compared to the offering of all the faithful at Mass.

Since Mary sublimely prefigures the whole Church, her offering at Calvary must not only be active but must also resemble Christ's own sacrifice. Thus, her sacrifice is 'interior,' concerning her sentiments and dispositions to accomplish God's will, as well as 'exterior,' concerning the immolation of her very self. Christ immolated his will and his body. Mary offers in Christ her maternal obedience and her whole existence as woman and mother. Her sacrifice does not multiply the sacrifice of Christ—neither does Holy Mass—but only accidentally perfects it by her human union and collaboration. In fact, no salvation is possible without a personal collaboration in our redemption. Mary is the unique Co-Redemptrix. Through her and in her we can learn how to become co-redeemers in Christ. If St. Paul had to suffer to make up all that was lacking in Christ for the sake of his body, the Church (see Col 1:24), how much more did Mary, who was one with Christ?

However, the sacrifice par excellence is Christ the Lamb of God. There is only one sacrifice of salvation, but this one sacrifice had two actors at Calvary: Jesus and Mary; Jesus unites his Mother intimately to Himself. The Mother at Calvary is a bridge to the Church. Through her active participation in offering Christ, the Church is able to collaborate in the offering of the same sacrifice and in being offered by Christ through the same sacrificial action. The High Priest draws Our Lady near to Him in order to later have the collaboration of the Church in sacramentally offering the same sacrifice at Mass. Mary stands at Calvary, and throughout Christ's life, as the unique participant in our Redemption. Thus, the sacrificial action of Mary at Calvary, as the *apex* of her ministry at Christ's side, is essential to discern Her unique sacerdotal cooperation with Christ.

Vatican II, summarizing the previous Magisterium on this soteriological account says that Our Lady

> faithfully persevered in her union with her Son unto the cross where she stood, in keeping with the divine plan, grieving exceedingly with her only begotten Son, uniting herself with a maternal heart with His sacrifice, and lovingly consenting to the immolation of this Victim which she herself had brought forth (LG 58).

This magisterial text contains two important terms related to Mary's priestly ministry. First, Mary *united* herself with the sacrifice of Christ and, secondly, gave her *consent* to the immolation of the divine Victim. She did what no other human being, even a priest, can do. Only her *Fiat* cooperated to structure inwardly the same sacrifice of Christ, and her consent was the effect of her obedience to the will of God. Her consent was part of that sacrifice. The Church, therefore, has received from Christ through Mary the command of offering that same sacrifice sacramentally through the ministerial cooperation of priests, who sanctify the offerings of lay people.

4. MARY'S UNIQUE PRIESTHOOD

Mary's uniqueness as Co-Redemptrix shines forth through her singular participation in the priesthood of Christ. Since the whole Church shares in the priesthood of Christ, Mary too has a part. She does not share in the common priesthood of all the baptized, because, more than anyone else, she accomplished *with* Christ and *in* Christ the mystery of our Redemption. She was not baptized since she was immaculately conceived. She was redeemed by Christ, but in a unique manner; she was preserved from original sin so she could become Christ's co-worker in our common salvation, i.e., in mankind's deliverance from sin after falling in Adam and Eve.

Our Lady shares in the priesthood of Christ in a greater and higher way than all the baptized. All Christians can play an active

A 'Sacerdotal People of God'

role by bearing witness to Christ with their good works and uniting themselves with the oblation of the Holy Eucharist at Mass because of Mary. In her, they receive an outstanding model of cooperation with Christ. Moreover, Our Lady's personal cooperation in the work of Redemption lets the whole Church and each baptized person cooperate actively with Christ. Through her maternal attitude in being one with Christ and remaining by his side during all her life, she transmits the joy and the power of being Christ's witness to the faithful.

In the ministerial priesthood, she has a special role as well. She is not a priest but something greater and higher. Our Lady is greater than any priest. Priests offer the sacrifice of Calvary under the sacramental species of bread and wine after Jesus' ascent into Heaven, during the time of application of the merits of the Redemption. Mary, however, participated in Christ's sacrifice during his life, and especially at Calvary when Redemption as such was accomplished.

Our Lady precedes the priests and the faithful, for whom she is the living bond with Christ and with his salvation. We can understand Our Lady's priesthood by looking at Christ directly. To understand the priesthood of the Church, we must contemplate both Christ's and Mary's priesthood. For this reason, Our Lady's priesthood is a 'maternal mediation' in Christ, bringing forth into the world the 'sacrifice of communion' by which we are saved. Christ and Mary, the new Adam and the new Eve, are the two actors of our salvation. Mary exercises her priesthood because, in Christ, she collaborates in offering the sacrifice of Redemption and, as Mediatrix, she is the bridge between Christ and us, reconciling us with Christ and her Son with us.

It is not necessary to speak about Mary as a priest. Such a title could easily be misunderstood. The title *Virgo Sacerdos* together with a holy card of Our Lady dressed in priestly vestments (diaconal more precisely) was distributed at the time of Pius X, who, in 1906 gave an indulgence for the prayer composed by Cardinal Vannutelli. A double intervention of the Holy Office forbade first the spread of the image depicting Our Lady as a priest, in 1916, and then in 1927, with a letter to the Bishop of Adria (Italy), the devotion itself to Our Lady Priest, due to an misunderstanding of the ministerial priesthood caused by a theological article published in a review of that diocese.

The problem arose especially from the spread of the image and, consequently, from the Marian title, which, translated into French, was addressing Our Lady as *Vierge Prêtre, Virgin Priest*. Both the title and the devotion to Our Lady *Virgo Sacerdos* originated in Belgium thanks to the spiritual work of Bl. Marie Deluil Martiny (1841-1884), founder of the religious Institute of the Daughters of the Sacred Heart, whose spirituality is to live for the sanctification of priests, offering themselves in reparation for all the outrages against Jesus in the Sacred Host. Our Lady as the *Virgin Offering* was an inspirational model for this new religious Institute. *Vierge Prêtre* alluded to Mary as Priest, although the intention and the theology behind it were sound and preserved this new spirituality from erroneously considering Mary as an ordained priest. The title was pointing to Mary as a co-worker in our Redemption, on who carried out priestly functions, such as generating, nourishing and offering the Victim for our salvation.

The Latin title *Virgo Sacerdos* is unambiguous because *sacerdos*, *sacerdotium* is an analogical term, whose root is the priesthood of Christ and can be applied either to ordained ministers (priests) or to lay people on account of their baptism (common priesthood). Its translation into vernacular languages (such as French), however, creates ambiguity, allowing the ordained priesthood to be confused with the baptismal one. The beginning of the twentieth century, when priestly-Marian spirituality was flowering, was not prepared to receive the theology correctly, due to a lack of theology of the priesthood focused on its wider layout, starting with Christ the High Priest. In other words, priesthood at that time was exclusive to the sacrament of Holy Orders. With *Lumen Gentium* at Vatican II the priesthood of all the faithful was seen from a specific angle, originating with Christ as priest, king, and prophet. To speak of Mary as the one *participating* in Christ's priesthood from this background is not only accurate but also clear and fitting. Mary as *Virgo Sacerdos* is defined as very precise boundaries, when kept in the original Latin.

Unfortunately, confusion still surrounds the issue, for some teach that traditionally there are reasons to call Mary a priest.

A 'Sacerdotal People of God'

Hence, "devotion to Mary priest is a 'latent' tradition that implies that women can be ordained." These are essentially two pillars of the Wijngaards Institute for Catholic Research (see their website www.womenpriests.org), which promotes the ordination of women to the ministerial priesthood in the catholic milieu. Interestingly, one of the primary efforts put into this reaffirmation of women's equal dignity with men, i.e., women becoming priests or even popes, revolves around an ambiguous reading of Mary's ministry. While devotion to Mary in her sacerdotal functions at the side of Christ, her Son, is established in tradition, it was never claimed that Christ ordained Mary a priest. Consequently, devotion to Mary Priest, i.e., the one who fulfils her priestly-maternal task, can never justify the ordination of women to the priesthood.

This question highlights two theological issues. Firstly, the word "priest" is read as a one-way term. Willingly avoiding its analogical meaning, it is taken as univocal in reference to the ministerial priesthood only. We should remember the critical progress with Vatican II to avoid transforming the Church into an exclusively clerical body, where lay people are easily transformed into clergy, and vice-versa clergy quickly become secularised and hide their status. Secondly, devotion to Mary Priest, rather than opening the door to women's ordination, testifies to the great love and self-oblation of Mary for her Son's salvific mystery. Our Lady personifies the Church as bride and as body, but not as head. The only head of the Church is Christ, and she is not a substitute for Him. She is at his side as co-worker. Complementarity between man and woman reaches its apex in this relationship.

For all these reasons, it is fitting to see Our Lady as the unique co-operator in Christ. Her unique participation in the Redemption models the Church, whether in her ministerial or in her common priesthood. To priests, Mary is the Mother who collaborates with Christ and gives them a pattern in offering not only the divine Victim but also themselves with it. To all baptized people, Mary is the Mother who leads them to supernatural life and enables the Church as an entire mystical body to receive grace and life from the Head in order to be active in responding to all the duties of the Christian vocation.

The priest is always the head of the Body and the faithful are the members. Mary is a member of the Church—an outstanding member—but, in relation to her Immaculate Conception, she is greater than the whole body. While she does not act *in persona Christi*, i.e., does not sacramentally personify Christ as head of the Church as only a priest can do, she brings forth Christ into the world. In giving her flesh to Him she let the sacrifice of Calvary happen. She simply stays with Christ above and behind human collaboration and contributes to generating supernatural life in both shepherds and flock, priests and faithful. In Christ *through* Mary, our Mother Church is saved and salvific. All men of good will, always through her, can have a salvific encounter with their Lord.

CONCLUSION

At the end of this reflection, we recall what Benedict XVI said during a General Audience (August 12, 2009) dedicated to Mary, Mother of the Priest: "... sacrifice, priesthood and Incarnation go together and Mary is at the heart of this mystery." Priesthood is essentially mediation between God and man, and sacrifice is the very apex of this mediation, its own salvific completion. Our Lady is Mediatrix, who in Christ offered that sacrifice of salvation and with it offered herself. The sacrifice which gave us life was kept in her. She is its treasurer.

We will conclude with the splendid words of Theofanis Nicene (bishop of Nicea, † 1381), underlining the unity of altar, victim, and priesthood, a unity entrusted to Our Lady:

> Jesus Christ disposed and prepared the heart of the Virgin so as to become the altar of his sacrifice. Where could the sacrifice of the New Law be collocated if not in She from whom the victim was born and was nourished? As the divinization of the Christian will proceed always from Mary, in the same way the sacrifice of the New Testament will repose eternally offered and accepted in Our Lady's heart.[2]

---

[2] *Sermo in Sanctissimam Deiparam*, ed. M. Jugie, Rome 1935, pp. 147–149.

ABOUT THE AUTHOR

Fr Serafino M. Lanzetta STD is resident in the Diocese of Portsmouth (England) where he exercises his priestly ministry. He is lecturer in Dogmatic Theology at the Theological Faculty of Lugano (Switzerland) and editor-in chief of the Theological Journal *Fides Catholica*. He has facilitated the organisation of several Theological Conferences—the last one on The Fatima Message in its 100th Anniversary, and has written for *L'Osservatore Romano*. His published works include his post-doctoral habilitation, *Vatican II, a Pastoral Council: Hermeneutics of Council Teaching* (Gracewing, 2016), and *Fatima at the Heart of the Church: God's Vision of History and Oblative Spirituality* (2018).

www.ingramcontent.com/pod-product-compliance
Lightning Source LLC
Chambersburg PA
CBHW021427070526
44577CB00001B/90